Festive Desserts

FEATURING RECIPES FROM THE BEST-SELLING BEAUTIFUL COOKBOOKS

Festive Desserts

Text by Norman Kolpas

CollinsPublishersSanFrancisco

A Division of HarperCollins*Publishers*

First published in USA 1996 by Collins Publishers San Francisco
1160 Battery Street, San Francisco, CA 94111-1213
HarperCollins Web Site: http://www.harpercollins.com

Produced by Weldon Owen Inc.

Editor: Hannah Rahill
Text Author: Norman Kolpas
Copy Editor: Judith Dunham
Proofreaders: Ken DellaPenta and Sharilyn Hovind
Index: Ken DellaPenta
Design Concept: John Bull
Design: Kari Perin, Perin + Perin
Series Editor: Meesha Halm
Production: Jenny Collins, Kristen Wurz

Cover Photograph: Allan Rosenberg

Library of Congress Cataloging-in-Publication Data
Kolpas, Norman.
Festive desserts / text by Norman Kolpas.
p. cm. — (Easy entertaining)
Includes index.
ISBN 0-00-225089-6
1. Desserts. 2. Entertaining.
I. Title. II. Series: Easy entertaining series.
TX773.K583 1996
641.8'6—dc 20   CIP 96-15174

Manufactured by Toppan
Printed in China
1 3 5 7 9 10 8 6 4 2

Front cover: Mile-High Plum Cake (recipe page 22)
Page 1: Chocolate Zucchini Cake (recipe page 23)
Page 2: Poached Pears with Chocolate Sabayon (recipe page 80)

CONTENTS

INTRODUCTION

"'Tis the dessert that graces all the feast," an anonymous philosopher long ago observed. Translated into modern terms, this means that no course of a menu makes a party more festive than dessert.

Of course, when you entertain, you want to make the entire meal memorable from first bite to last. If you lead a busy life, time may not be an ingredient that you have in great supply to lavish on every single course. So for the appetizer, entrée and side dishes, you can turn to simple, tasty, reliable recipes. But for dessert—that's where you'll still want to make a special effort, whether on a luxuriously frosted layer cake or a pie filled with succulent seasonal fruit or an imaginative pairing of sorbet and cookies.

The work you put into a dessert brings a manifold payoff, as your guests conclude the meal with the very best impression you have to offer. So great is the impression dessert can make that many savvy hosts and hostesses eliminate the other courses of the meal altogether and decide to entertain their guests with the enticing invitation "Come on over for dessert."

However you use desserts in your own entertaining, this book aims to make their preparation and presentation as smooth and successful as possible. On the following pages, you'll find a concise, comprehensive guide to essential dessert-making ingredients, along with brief, easy-to-follow instructions on such basic procedures as baking cakes and preparing pie and tart pastry. The guidelines and helpful tips for presenting, serving

and entertaining with desserts will allow you to spend a minimum of effort to create a maximum effect at any occasion, be it a casual supper, an afternoon tea or shower, a formal dinner party or a dessert extravaganza.

These introductory pages are followed by four chapters with forty-three recipes for festive desserts. The first features cakes, without a doubt the kind of dessert most people associate with such celebratory occasions as a birthday or anniversary. You'll discover these luscious confections—such as Easy Chocolate Cake, a chocolate lover's fantasy come true, and Peach Brandy Pound Cake with Lemon Verbena, an imaginative variation on an old-fashioned favorite—are easily made, sometimes hours in advance of your guests' arrival. Next come pies and tarts, ranging from homey constructions of apples to gala assemblies of mixed summer berries and sour cream.

Two kinds of desserts that are often served in tandem—iced desserts and cookies—share the following chapter, ready to grace occasions as varied as a backyard barbecue and a fancy tea or shower. Last come "grand finales." Including a Pavlova, poached pears, cream puffs, crêpes and French custard, this chapter offers an assortment of ever-popular desserts that are guaranteed to excite comment and leave your guests with a dazzling last impression.

As you browse through these recipes and admire the photographs brimming with presentation ideas, you'll notice abundant instructions for how to prepare recipes at least partially in advance, as well as suggestions for alternative and substitute ingredients. The goal is to make entertaining with desserts easy and enjoyable and to inspire you to make your parties more festive than ever before.

THE WELL-STOCKED PANTRY

If you keep on hand in your kitchen cupboard or pantry and refrigerator a good supply of the staples listed below, virtually any of the dessert recipes in this book will be easily within your grasp. Only a brief trip to the market will be necessary to pick up special or perishable items. Also included are basic techniques relating to the preparation of cakes, chocolate, coconut, eggs, nuts, and pie and tart pastry.

BAKING POWDER
Used to leaven batters and doughs, this commercial product packaged in airtight tins combines baking soda; an acid such as cream of tartar, which reacts with the baking soda, causing it to release carbon dioxide gas; and a starch such as cornstarch to help keep the mixture dry. The most commonly used type is double-acting baking powder, which releases gas first when mixed with liquid and again when in contact with heat. Store in a cool, dry place and replace every 4 months.

BAKING SODA
This active component of baking powder, also known as bicarbonate of soda, is used on its own to leaven batters and doughs when an acidic ingredient such as buttermilk, yogurt or citrus juice is also present. Store in an airtight container in a cool, dry place and replace every 6 months.

BUTTER
Unsalted, or "sweet," butter is recommended for most dessert making because it lacks salt and is inevitably fresher and purer in flavor. Left in its original wrapping, unsalted butter will keep in the refrigerator for up to 2 weeks, salted butter for 3 weeks. Wrapped airtight, butter can be frozen for up to 4 months.

BUTTERMILK
A tangy enrichment to cake batters and dessert fillings, this thick, creamy liquid is cultured from low-fat or nonfat milk. Purchase buttermilk well in advance of the pull date printed on the container and store in the refrigerator for up to 4 days.

CAKES
Most of the cakes in this book rely on time-tested techniques and equipment, the fundamentals of which are reviewed here.

Choosing Cake Pans: Use a cake pan of the dimensions called for in a particular recipe; a different-sized pan will affect the baking time and the final results. Seek out cake pans in unusual, decorative shapes—hearts or Christmas trees, for example—for special occasions.

Preparing Cake Pans: Although specific recipes differ in how to prepare a cake pan before the batter is added, greasing and flouring a pan are the most common ways of preventing a cake from sticking. Evenly smear a thin coating of softened butter over the entire bottom and sides. Add a heaping spoonful of flour and tilt and shake the pan to dust the buttered surfaces evenly; invert the pan and tap gently to remove any excess flour.

Testing Cakes for Doneness: When a recipe gives a time range for baking, begin testing at the earliest moment a cake could be done. It should look evenly well risen. If it is a white or yellow cake, the surface should be golden brown. Depending on the recipe, the cake might shrink slightly from the sides of the pan. When a wooden toothpick or skewer is inserted into the center, it should come out clean, with no batter adhering.

Unmolding Cakes: Whether a recipe calls for a cake to cool in its pan or be unmolded while still hot, the same technique applies. Place a wire rack over the cake pan and grip pan and rack securely together with both hands, using pot holders if the pan is still hot. Invert pan and rack, then carefully lift off the cake pan. If the cake will not unmold, run a small, thin-bladed knife around its sides and repeat.

Frosting and Glazing Cakes: Use an icing spatula—a long, thin, flexible flat metal blade with a rounded end and dull edges—to spread both thin glazes and thick frostings on cakes.

CHOCOLATE

One of the most popular dessert ingredients, chocolate finds its way into recipes in many different forms, including the following products used in this book. Seek out the best-quality chocolate you can find. Many experienced dessert cooks favor Swiss, Belgian, French or Italian products. Blocks or bars of solid chocolate are often scored or divided into convenient 1-ounce segments. Store solid chocolate for up to 4 months and cocoa indefinitely in a cool, dry place.

Unsweetened Chocolate: Blocks of bitter chocolate are made from pure, ground roasted cocoa beans. A source of intense flavor, it is used in combination with sugar, butter and milk.

Bittersweet Chocolate: Used for both eating and cooking, this variety combines bitter ground chocolate with additional cocoa butter and sugar.

Semisweet Chocolate: This eating and cooking chocolate is usually a little sweeter than bittersweet chocolate, with which it is interchangeable. Semisweet is often sold in the form of chocolate chips.

Unsweetened Cocoa Powder: This fine, light brown powder has a rich chocolate flavor and is fairly acidic, reacting well with baking soda to leaven cakes and other baked goods.

White Chocolate: This eating or cooking product highlights the richness and subtle hint of chocolate flavor found in the ivory-colored butter extracted from cocoa solids, which is combined with powdered milk, sugar and sometimes vanilla. Seek out products made from pure cocoa butter, without the use of coconut oil or vegetable oil.

Making Chocolate Curls: Wafer-thin curls of dark or white chocolate make lovely garnishes for desserts. Leave a large block of good-quality chocolate at room temperature until it feels slightly softened. Drag a swivel-bladed vegetable peeler or the sharp blade of a large knife across the surface to form the curls. Store the curls in a cool place if not using immediately.

COCONUT

Sold in plastic bags or cans, shredded or flaked, coconut adds rich flavor and intriguing texture to desserts. It is available unsweetened or sweetened. Store in an airtight container in a cool, dry place for up to 4 months.

Toasting Coconut: Baking coconut before using it as an ingredient, topping or garnish enhances its flavor, color and texture. Spread the coconut evenly on a baking sheet and bake in a 350°F oven, stirring occasionally, until golden, 10–20 minutes depending on its moisture content.

CORN SYRUP

Extracted from corn, this relatively flavorless sweetener comes in both light-colored and dark-colored forms. Store tightly capped bottles of corn syrup in a cool, dry place.

CORNSTARCH

This fine, starchy, flavorless powder ground from the white hearts of corn kernels is used as a thickening agent in some desserts. Store indefinitely in a cool, dry place.

CREAM

The most commonly used form of cream for dessert making, labeled "heavy" or "whipping" cream, has a butterfat content of no less than 36 percent. Avoid using products labeled "ultra pasteurized," because they may also contain stabilizers and emulsifiers; these will not have as pure a flavor, and the heavy varieties will not whip as well. Half-and-half, which contains between 10.5 and 18 percent butterfat, cannot be whipped. Purchase cream well in advance of the pull date printed on the container and store in the refrigerator for up to 1 week.

Preparing Whipped Cream: Use a deep bowl that is large enough to allow the cream to double in volume. Chill the bowl and beaters as well as the cream ahead of time. With an electric mixer set on medium speed—or with a wire balloon whisk—beat until the cream forms soft or stiff peaks when the beaters are lifted. Sugar or other sweeteners or flavorings can be added while beating. Whipped cream can be covered and refrigerated for up to 4 hours, then whipped lightly before using. One cup of heavy cream yields about 2 cups of whipped cream.

CREAM CHEESE

Made from cream and milk, this smooth, thick, mild spread contributes richness and smoothness to desserts. Low-fat and nonfat, as well as regular, cream cheese are available. Store in the refrigerator for up to 1 week.

CREAM OF TARTAR

A residue of the wine-making process, this acidic powder is used to stabilize egg whites during beating. Combined with baking soda in commercial baking powder, it also plays a role in leavening doughs and batters. Store cream of tartar in its original packaging in a cool, dry place.

CRÈME FRAÎCHE

This French cultured cream has a tangy flavor to complement its richness, making it an intriguing enrichment for desserts. It is sold in specialty-food shops and well-stocked markets. Store in the refrigerator for up to 1 week.

Making Crème Fraîche: In a small bowl, combine 1 cup heavy cream and 2 tablespoons buttermilk. Cover and let stand at room temperature until thick, 8–24 hours. Refrigerate for up to 10 days. Alternatively, in a small bowl, stir together $1/3$ cup heavy cream and $2/3$ cup sour cream. Cover and refrigerate for up to 2 days.

EGGS

Eggs are commonly sold in a range of sizes. For the recipes in this book, use large eggs.

Separating Eggs: Work over a small bowl. This enables you to set aside any eggs with accidentally broken yolks, which would interfere with beating the whites properly. Crack the middle of the shell against the edge of the bowl, then gently break the shell open. Carefully pass the yolk back and forth between the shell halves while allowing the clear egg white to drip into the bowl. Transfer the white to a separate bowl and place the yolk in another bowl.

Beating Egg Whites: For the best results, the whites should stand at room temperature for 30 minutes before beating. Use an unlined copper bowl, which, through a harmless chemical re-action, causes the whites to adhere to it, allowing more air to be beaten into them. Alternatively, use a stainless steel bowl and add 1/8 teaspoon cream of tartar for each 2 egg whites to help stabilize them. Make sure that the bowl is large and deep enough to allow the whites to triple in volume, and that both bowl and beaters are clean and dry. With an electric mixer set on medium speed—or with a wire balloon whisk—beat the whites in broad strokes. Whites beaten to the soft-peak stage will form peaks that droop when the beater is lifted out; stiff peaks remain firm and pointed when the beater is lifted. Sugar and vanilla can be added while beating to make meringue. Beaten whites should be used immediately.

Folding Egg Whites: When other ingredients or mixtures are combined with beaten egg whites, their weight can deflate the whites. To prevent this, stir about one-fourth of the whites into the other mixture to lighten them, using a rubber spatula to repeatedly cut straight down through the center of the bowl and under and up the side until thoroughly combined. Then add that mixture to the remaining beaten whites and continue folding until the ingredients are evenly combined.

EVAPORATED MILK

Made by evaporating 60 percent of the water content of milk, this canned product—also called condensed milk—is used to enrich baked goods, fillings and sauces. Low-fat evaporated milk, regular evaporated milk and sweetened condensed milk are available. Store unopened cans in a cool, dry place for up to 1 year. Leftover milk from opened cans should be trans-ferred to an airtight container and refrigerated for up to 4 days.

EXTRACTS

Extensively used as dessert flavorings, extracts are made by dissolving the essential oils of such ingredients as almonds, lemons, oranges and vanilla beans in an alcohol base. Avoid artificial flavorings and seek out products labeled "pure" or "natural." Store indefinitely in a cool, dry place.

FILO PASTRY

Also spelled phyllo, these large paper-thin pastry sheets are used in Greek and Middle Eastern desserts. Filo is sold frozen in boxes in Middle Eastern shops and in the freezer section of well-stocked supermarkets. Thaw the pastry in the refrigera-tor for 8 hours or overnight. The sheets dry out easily and can become brittle; open the package only after all the other ingre-dients for a recipe have been readied, and keep the sheets well covered with waxed paper or plastic wrap topped with a damp kitchen towel. Unopened filo can be stored in the freezer for up to 4 months or in the refrigerator for up to 3 weeks.

FLOUR

All-purpose flour blends flours from hard and soft wheats. Cake flour, also known as soft-wheat flour, yields more tender results for cake-making purposes. Store flour in an airtight container in a cool, dry place and replace after 6–8 months.

Sifting Flour: This simple technique passes flour, along with other dry ingredients, through a fine screen to lighten and loosen it and remove any lumps. Sifting can be accomplished with a fine-mesh sieve, its rim tapped by hand, or with a special sifter that has a handle that is squeezed to push the ingredients back and forth across a screen. The same technique can be used to apply a decorative dusting of confectioners' sugar or cocoa powder to a dessert.

FLOWERS AND LEAVES

Fragrant, attractively shaped and colorful flowers and leaves are used to flavor and decorate desserts. It is essential to choose only nontoxic fresh plants and flowers grown completely free of pesticides. Some well-stocked supermarkets sell small packages of such flowers, or you can grow simple specimens such as roses, violets, nasturtiums, calendula, fuchsia, marigolds, pansies, borage violas and scented geraniums. Candied flowers, used for garnishes, are available in specialty-food stores and gourmet cooking shops.

FRUIT

Naturally sweet, colorful and succulent, fresh and dried fruits are the very essence of dessert. For fresh fruit, find a market or produce shop that offers you the widest variety and best quality. For optimum flavor, texture and value, choose fruits that are at their seasonal peak. The following techniques are called for in the recipes in this volume.

Peeling Peaches and Nectarines: Immerse the fruit in boiling water for 20–30 seconds to loosen the skin. Let cool, then remove the skin with your fingers or a small knife.

Pitting Cherries: Use a special cherry pitter, which grips the cherry and pushes out the pit with a squeeze of the handle, leaving the fruit whole.

Dried and Candied Fruit

Many varieties of fruit are sun-dried, kiln-dried or saturated with sugar syrups to produce intense flavors and chewy textures that enhance many desserts. Raisins—dried grapes—are perhaps the most popular fruit of this type. The most common candied fruits are citron and orange peel, cherries and pineapple. Dates, the sweet, caramel brown fruit of the date palm tree, have a dense, sticky flesh that causes them to be grouped among candied fruits. Store dried and candied fruits in an airtight container in the refrigerator for up to 1 year.

GELATIN

Sold in envelopes, this unflavored product is used to contribute body to some desserts. Store indefinitely in a cool, dry place.

HERBS AND SPICES

Common sweet seasonings found in the spice and produce sections of well-stocked supermarkets are a source of lively flavor in dessert recipes. Fresh herb sprigs also make attractive garnishes. Store fresh herbs and spices, wrapped airtight, in the refrigerator for 4–6 days. Store spices and dried herbs in airtight containers in a cool, dry place for 6–8 months, then replace. The following are used in this book.

Herbs

Lemon thyme: This variety of the clean-tasting herb, used fresh or dried, has a refreshing lemony scent.

Lemon verbena: Possessing a strong lemon scent, this fresh herb should be used sparingly in desserts.

Mint: A refreshing complement to fruit, mint is used most often in its fresh form.

Rosemary: The strongly aromatic herb is used fresh or dried.

Spices

Cinnamon: This popular spice, the bark of a type of evergreen tree, is available in long, thin curls of bark—called cinnamon sticks—or finely ground.

Cloves: This East African spice has a rich, headily aromatic scent. It is used whole or finely ground.

Ginger: The rhizome of a tropical plant, ginger has a sweet flavor, almost hot in its intensity. It is used fresh, in crystallized or candied form, or dried and powdered.

Nutmeg: A popular baking spice, the hard, acorn-shaped pit of the fruit of the nutmeg tree is commonly sold ground. The best flavor is derived from freshly ground nutmeg. Buy the spice whole and grate it as needed on a fine nutmeg grater.

Vanilla Bean: Derived from the long, slender dried pods of a variety of orchid, this popular dessert flavoring is most often added in the form of an extract. Whole vanilla beans, of which the Madagascar variety is considered superior, yield intense, pure flavor.

HONEY
Honey is made from the nectar of blossoms and reflects the taste, aroma and color of its particular source. Mild clover or orange blossom varieties are generally preferred for all-purpose use. Distinctive honeys may be used to contribute special flavor. Store indefinitely in a cool, dry place.

LIQUEURS AND SPIRITS
A wide range of sweet liqueurs and dry spirits lend their distinctive flavors to dessert recipes. Seek out a well-stocked liquor store for the best selection. Store indefinitely at room temperature.

MASCARPONE CHEESE
Similar to cream cheese, this thick Italian cultured cream can be found in the cheese section of well-stocked supermarkets and in Italian delicatessens. Store in the refrigerator for up to 1 week.

MOLASSES
This thick liquid sweetening agent is a by-product of sugar refining. Two forms are commonly available: light, which has a mild flavor, and dark, which is stronger tasting but not as sweet. Store unopened molasses indefinitely in a cool, dry place. Refrigerate after opening.

NUTS
Almonds, hazelnuts, pecans, walnuts—nearly every nut variety can be kept on hand for use in cakes, pies, tart crusts and cookies. Store unshelled nuts in a cool, dry place for 6 months. Store shelled nuts in an airtight container in the refrigerator for 6 months or in the freezer for 1 year.

Toasting Nuts: Place shelled nuts in a heavy, dry frying pan over medium-low heat and stir gently until lightly browned and fragrant, 2–5 minutes; watch closely to guard against burning. Alternatively, place the nuts on a baking sheet and toast in a 350°F oven, stirring occasionally, until browned and fragrant, 5–10 minutes.

Grinding Nuts: Place the nuts in a food processor fitted with the metal blade or in a blender. Pulse on-off until the nuts are ground to the desired consistency. Do not overprocess, or the nuts will release their oils and produce nut butter.

ORANGEFLOWER WATER
This intense flavoring distilled from orange blossoms is popular in Middle Eastern and Mediterranean desserts. It is sold in Middle Eastern markets and the gourmet section of well-stocked supermarkets. Store indefinitely in a cool, dry place.

PASTRY

Several techniques will facilitate the preparation of the tart and pie pastry shells called for in this book. If you're short on time, ready-to-bake shells can be found in the refrigerator or freezer section of well-stocked supermarkets.

Preparing Pastry in a Food Processor: In a food processor fitted with the metal blade, combine the dry ingredients and pulse several times to mix. Add the butter or other fat and pulse until the mixture resembles coarse crumbs. Add the liquid, a little at a time, pulsing after each addition, just until the pastry forms a rough, damp mass. Using your hands, gather together the dough and chill or use as directed.

Rolling Out Pastry: Dust a work surface evenly with flour. Place the round of dough on it and, using a flour-dusted rolling pin, roll out the dough to a circle about 2 inches wider than the diameter of the pie or tart pan. Loosely roll up the dough around the rolling pin, then unroll it onto the pan and pat into place.

ROSEWATER

An intense flavoring distilled from rose petals, rosewater is popular in Middle Eastern and Mediterranean desserts. It is sold in Middle Eastern shops and the gourmet sections of well-stocked supermarkets. Store indefinitely in a cool, dry place.

SOUR CREAM

This dairy product cultured from sweet cream has a tangy acidity that makes it a distinctive enrichment in desserts. Store in the refrigerator for up to 1 week.

SUGAR

Various forms of sugar are used for dessert making. Store indefinitely in an airtight container in a cool, dry place.

Brown Sugar: Granulated sugar is combined with rich-tasting molasses of differing varieties to produce golden, light or dark brown sugar.

Confectioners' Sugar: Also known as powdered sugar or icing sugar, this pure white sugar has been ground to a very fine consistency for quick dissolving and for use as a decoration. It often includes a little cornstarch to prevent caking.

Granulated Sugar: This is the most standard, widely used form of pure white sugar.

Superfine Sugar: This form of granulated sugar has been ground to an extra-fine consistency for quick dissolving.

Making Vanilla Sugar: Take a fresh whole vanilla bean or a used one that has been rinsed off and dried. With a sharp knife, split it in half lengthwise and bury it in granulated, superfine or confectioners' sugar placed in a tightly covered jar. After a few days, the sugar will have absorbed the vanilla flavor.

VEGETABLE SHORTENING

This solid form of vegetable fat is used in doughs to "shorten" the flour, making it flakier and more tender. Store in the refrigerator for 3–4 weeks or in the freezer for up to 6 months.

ZEST

The outermost rind of citrus fruits, brightly colored zest contains aromatic oils that add spark to many desserts. When a recipe calls for zest, use only the colored part of the rind, avoiding the bitter white pith beneath.

Grating Zest: Use the fine holes of a handheld grater or the sharp-edged holes of a special tool known as a citrus zester. Alternatively, remove the zest in strips with a swivel-bladed vegetable peeler and cut into thin slivers.

THE ART OF PRESENTATION

By the very nature of their ingredients, desserts look festive: the jewel-like colors and contours of fresh fruit, the ivory richness of cream, the intriguing sheen and shapes of nuts, the deep brown luster of chocolate. The recipes here have been chosen with an eye toward attractiveness in the way they are composed and presented.

As the instructions and photographs in this book only begin to suggest, you can do even more not only to present desserts with festive flair but also to make them unique expressions of your own style and approach to entertaining.

Such creativity begins with the dishes in which you prepare and present desserts. Consider, for instance, cakes baked in tube or Bundt pans, such as Coffee Crunch Cake (page 25) or Peach Brandy Pound Cake (page 26). Seek out another interestingly faceted pan that meets the general specifications of the recipe, and the resulting cake gains another dimension of appeal. Likewise, pans in the form of hearts or other fanciful shapes may be substituted for round cake pans of similar volume and depth. Some pies and tarts may be prepared in attractively patterned ceramic bakeware that is appropriate to take from oven to table.

Most desserts, though, gain distinction from being transferred to attractive serving dishes for presentation. Classic pedestal-style cake stands literally elevate a cake. Individual cut-glass dishes make sorbets and ice creams sparkle. A thoughtfully chosen platter can mean the difference between a dessert that looks humdrum and one that is eye-catching. Survey all your serving pieces, then select the one that best complements the form and color of the dessert you plan to offer, as well as

underscores the theme and style of the event. To whatever extent is practical, use the same considerations when choosing individual serving dishes or plates, making sure that you have enough for each guest, along with the requisite dessert forks or spoons.

Give thought to garnishing the dessert. You'll find plenty of ideas throughout this book and many are interchangeable. Use a sieve or sifter to dust confectioners' sugar or cocoa powder over the surface of a dessert. Add a pattern by placing a paper doily or a stencil on top before you dust, then carefully lift it off. Colorful blossoms or distinctively shaped leaves create a pretty effect when placed around or on top of desserts; just make sure they come from nontoxic plants and have been grown pesticide-free. Chocolate curls (page 10), plump berries, nuts, mint sprigs, strips of citrus zest, dollops of whipped cream—each of these, and others your own imagination might devise—can enhance the spirit of festivity.

The occasion itself will dictate the effect you wish to achieve. When planning a dessert for any party, however large or small, casual or formal, give careful thought to what kind of recipe would work best. Consider the style of the event and whether it calls for something understated or impressive, simple or elaborate. If the event is a formal one, guests will not appreciate desserts that, however delicious, would be easy to spill on their dressy clothes. Whether the occasion is a buffet or sit-down meal, the rest of the menu will influence your choice— a heavy main course is best followed by a light dessert, while a light meal lets guests feel less guilty about indulging themselves in something rich. If you prepare a fruit-based dessert,

you'll want to choose fruits that are at their seasonal peak. Of equal importance is how much time your own schedule and the rest of the menu will let you spend on dessert preparation.

You might wish to devote the party to desserts alone. Desserts are ideal for an afternoon or after-dinner gathering. As a basis for planning, remember that guests are likely to try small servings of two or three different items. Multiply accordingly and add one more dessert for good measure. Be sure to offer a varied selection of different types of desserts, kinds of ingredients and flavors, and richer and lighter items.

Clear the dining table, a sideboard or a kitchen counter to present all the desserts together. Or, to encourage guests to wander and mingle, set up in different parts of your home separate stations for each dessert, complete with stacks of plates, cutlery and napkins. Because the desserts are likely to stay out in the open for some time, plan how you can best keep them in peak condition. A large batch of ice cream, for example, can be presented in a bowl set inside a larger bowl filled with crushed ice. A warm sauce such as Chocolate Sabayon (page 80) can be kept at optimum temperature in a chafing dish or on a hot plate.

With any dessert, whether offered on its own or as part of a buffet, hot coffee or tea is always appropriate. You might also wish to offer a liqueur or brandy. Borrowing a tradition common in Europe and the Middle East, it's a good idea to have pitchers of cold water and small glasses on hand, to counterbalance the sweetness and cleanse guests' palates for their next delicious taste.

CAKES

"If I knew you were coming," goes the old song, "I'd have baked a cake." Such is the power of a cake to make any occasion, from a friend's unexpected visit to a casual tea party to a gala birthday dinner, seem all the more special.

The eight cake recipes that follow cover all the entertaining bases, with many of them capable of playing multiple positions. Coconut Cake with Lemon Curd Filling has the right light touch to star at an afternoon tea or could be the dream-come-true birthday cake for a coconut-loving guest of honor. You can just as easily imagine Summer Berry Shortcake at a family-style Sunday dinner as at a gala backyard barbecue.

Not only are cakes versatile, they are surprisingly easy to make. Surprising, because to the casual observer they seem to be complex constructions of layers, fillings, frostings and garnishes. But most cake batters are prepared fairly quickly, as are their embellishments, and little effort is involved in putting them together.

Once made, most of the cakes in this chapter also keep fairly well for a day or two, if properly stored to safeguard their moistness. This means you can do the work well in advance of any festive occasion.

Mile-High Plum Cake (recipe page 22)

1¹/₂ lb (750 g) purple plums,
   pitted and cut into quarters

2 tablespoons water

3 cups (1¹/₂ lb/750 g)
   granulated sugar

¹/₂ teaspoon ground cinnamon

³/₄ cup (6 oz/185 g) unsalted
   butter

1 teaspoon vanilla extract
   (essence)

4 teaspoons grated orange zest

3 cups (15 oz/470 g) flour

1 tablespoon baking powder

¹/₄ teaspoon salt

1 cup (8 fl oz/250 ml) milk

6 egg whites

1¹/₂ cups (12 fl oz/375 ml)
   heavy (double) cream

¹/₄ cup (1 oz/30 g) sifted
   confectioners' (icing) sugar

3 tablespoons orange juice

pansy blossoms (see page 13;
   optional)

MILE-HIGH PLUM CAKE

*You can make and refrigerate this impressive cake up to a day ahead of serving.
The purple plums it calls for are also known as prune plums; you can substitute
other plum varieties, peaches or nectarines. (photograph pages 20–21)*

To make the plum compote, place the plums in a large saucepan, add the
water and sprinkle with 1 cup (8 oz/250 g) of the sugar and the cinnamon.
Cook over medium heat until the plums release some juice, then cover and
cook for 15 minutes. Uncover and cook until the plums have thickened to a
jamlike consistency, about 10 minutes. Let cool.

To make the cake, preheat an oven to 350°F (180°C). Butter and flour three
8-in (20-cm) round cake pans. In a large bowl, cream the butter and 1¹/₂ cups
(12 oz/375 g) of the remaining sugar. Add the vanilla and 2 teaspoons of the
orange zest. Sift the flour, baking powder and salt into a medium bowl. Add
the dry ingredients to the creamed mixture alternately with the milk, stirring
until smooth. In a large bowl, whip the egg whites until soft peaks form, then
sprinkle in the remaining ¹/₂ cup (4 oz/125 g) sugar and beat until stiff but
not dry. Mix one-fourth of the whites into the cake batter, then gently fold in
the remaining whites. Divide the batter evenly among the prepared cake pans.
Top each cake with ¹/₄ cup (2 fl oz/60 ml) of the plum compote. Bake until a
toothpick inserted into the cakes comes out clean, about 30 minutes. Cool in
the pans for 5 minutes, then remove and let cool on a rack.

To make the orange whipped cream, in a medium bowl, whip the cream and
confectioners' sugar until soft peaks form. Whisk in the remaining 2 teaspoons
orange zest and orange juice.

To assemble the cake, set one layer on a serving plate and spread half of the
remaining plum compote over the top, followed by one-third of the orange
whipped cream. Top with a second layer of cake and repeat with the remaining plum compote and one-third of the orange whipped cream. Add the third
layer. Frost the top of the cake with the remaining orange whipped cream and
chill until ready to serve. Garnish with a ring of pansies, if desired.

SERVES 8–10

- $^1/_2$ cup (4 oz/125 g) unsalted butter, at room temperature

- $^1/_2$ cup (4 fl oz/125 ml) vegetable oil

- 1 cup (8 oz/250 g) granulated sugar

- $^1/_2$ cup ($3^1/_2$ oz/105 g) firmly packed brown sugar

- 2 eggs

- 1 teaspoon vanilla extract (essence)

- $^1/_2$ cup (4 fl oz/125 ml) buttermilk

- $^1/_2$ teaspoon ground cinnamon

- $^1/_2$ teaspoon salt

- $^1/_2$ teaspoon baking powder

- $^1/_2$ teaspoon baking soda (bicarbonate of soda)

- $2^1/_2$ cups ($12^1/_2$ oz/390 g) flour

- $^1/_4$ cup (1 oz/30 g) unsweetened cocoa powder

- $^1/_2$ cup (2 oz/60 g) chopped walnuts

- 2 cups (8 oz/250 g) grated zucchini (courgettes)

- 2 cups (12 oz/375 g) semisweet (plain) chocolate chips

- $^1/_4$ cup (2 fl oz/60 ml) heavy (double) cream

- 2 tablespoons strong coffee

CHOCOLATE ZUCCHINI CAKE

The combination may sound strange, but the concept behind it is no different than that of popular carrot cakes, with the zucchini providing exceptional moistness and interesting texture. Grated apple or carrot can be substituted for the zucchini. The cake, with its hint of spice and its mocha glaze, delights sophisticated chocolate lovers, for whom it makes a great treat on a birthday or other special occasion. It freezes exceptionally well. (photograph page 1)

Preheat an oven to 350°F (180°C). Butter a 10-in (25-cm) Bundt pan and dust with flour.

To make the cake, in a medium bowl, cream together the butter, oil and granulated and brown sugars. Beat in the eggs, vanilla and buttermilk until smooth. Sift the cinnamon, salt, baking powder, baking soda, flour and cocoa into a medium bowl. Gradually add the dry ingredients to the butter-sugar mixture and mix until incorporated. Stir in the walnuts, zucchini and 1 cup (6 oz/185 g) of the chocolate chips.

Pour the batter into the prepared pan. Bake until a toothpick inserted into the center comes out clean, about $1^1/_4$ hours. Cool the cake in the pan for about 5 minutes, then remove from the pan and place on a rack to cool.

To make the glaze, in a small saucepan over low heat, heat the remaining 1 cup (6 oz/185 g) chocolate chips, cream and coffee, stirring occasionally, until smooth and just melted. Pour over the cake. Let stand for 15 minutes before slicing into wedges and serving.

SERVES 12

1 cup (4 oz/125 g) cake
(soft-wheat) flour

3 cups (1¹/₂ lb/745 g)
granulated sugar

2 cups (16 fl oz/500 ml) egg whites
(about 13 eggs)

1¹/₂ teaspoons cream of tartar

3 teaspoons vanilla extract
(essence)

¹/₂ teaspoon salt

¹/₄ cup (2 fl oz/60 ml) strong coffee

¹/₂ cup (4 fl oz/125 ml) light
corn syrup

1 tablespoon baking soda
(bicarbonate of soda), sifted

3 cups (24 fl oz/750 ml) heavy
(double) cream

3 tablespoons nonfat dry milk
(milk powder)

¹/₄ cup (1 oz/30 g) confectioners'
(icing) sugar

COFFEE CRUNCH CAKE

This time-honored cake is simply an angel food cake frosted generously with whipped cream and coated with a brittle, crunchy coffee candy. If you are pressed for time, you could substitute a plain store-bought angel food cake or a sponge cake.

Preheat an oven to 375°F (190°C). To make the angel food cake, in a small bowl, combine the cake flour with ³/₄ cup (6 oz/185 g) of the granulated sugar and sift 3 times. In a large bowl, beat the egg whites for 1 minute. Add the cream of tartar, 1 teaspoon of the vanilla and the salt. Beat in ³/₄ cup (6 oz/ 185 g) of the granulated sugar, one tablespoon at a time. Beat until the whites form soft peaks. Sift about one-third of the flour-sugar mixture over the beaten whites and fold in until mostly incorporated. Sift half the remaining flour mixture on top and fold in until mostly incorporated, then sift on the last of the flour mixture and fold in until there are no unblended streaks.

Scoop the batter into an ungreased 10-in (25-cm) tube pan. Bake until a toothpick inserted into the cake comes out clean, 35–45 minutes. Cool upside down by placing the tube over the neck of a bottle. To remove the cake, insert a long, thin-bladed knife between the cake and the edge of the pan. Cut around the side and center tube. Gently ease the cake from the bottom.

To make the coffee candy, line the bottom and sides of a jelly-roll pan with foil. Combine the remaining 1¹/₂ cups (12 oz/375 g) sugar, coffee and corn syrup in a large saucepan. Bring to a boil over medium heat and cook to the hard-crack stage, 305°F (150°C) on a candy thermometer. Remove from the heat, add the baking soda and stir to combine; the mixture will pull away from the pot. Pour onto the foil-lined pan and let harden. Peel off the foil and break the candy into ¹/₂-in (12-mm) pieces. Store airtight until ready to use.

To make the icing, whip the cream with the dry milk, confectioners' sugar and remaining 2 teaspoons vanilla until the cream stands in peaks. Split the cake horizontally into 4 layers. Spread the cream between the layers, then frost the top and sides. Shortly before serving, sprinkle the candy all over the cake.

SERVES 12

1 cup (8 oz/250 g) unsalted
  butter, at room temperature

3 cups (1^1/$_2$ lb/750 g) sugar

6 eggs, at room temperature

3 cups (15 oz/470 g) flour

^{1}/$_4$ teaspoon salt

1 cup (8 oz/250 g) sour cream

1 teaspoon orange extract
  (essence)

^{1}/$_2$ teaspoon almond extract
  (essence)

^{1}/$_2$ teaspoon lemon extract
  (essence)

1 teaspoon vanilla extract
  (essence)

2 teaspoons light rum

^{1}/$_2$ cup (4 fl oz/125 ml)
  peach brandy

15 fresh lemon verbena leaves
  (see page 13)

fresh lemon verbena sprigs and
  begonia blossoms (see page 13)

PEACH BRANDY POUND CAKE WITH LEMON VERBENA

A morning kaffeeklatsch or afternoon tea becomes extra-special with this intriguing, fragrant cake. Lemon verbena, an herb with narrow, pointed green leaves and an intense lemon scent, covers the bottom of the cake pan so that when the cake is inverted the leaves are on top. Lemon geranium, lemon thyme, lemon balm or rose geranium would work equally well and would also make lovely garnishes for the cake plate.

Preheat an oven to 325°F (165°C). Butter a 10-in (25-cm) Bundt pan and dust with flour. In a large bowl, beat the butter and sugar until light and fluffy. Add the eggs, one at a time, beating well after each addition. In a medium bowl, stir together the flour and salt. Beat the flour mixture into the butter-sugar mixture alternately with the sour cream, in 3 additions each. Stir in the orange, almond, lemon and vanilla extracts, then add the rum and peach brandy.

Place the lemon verbena leaves on the bottom of the prepared pan, with the underside of the leaves facing up. Spoon the batter into the pan, being careful not to dislodge the leaves. Bake until a toothpick inserted into the center comes out clean, about 1^1/$_4$ hours.

Cool the cake for 10 minutes in the pan, then invert onto a rack to cool completely. Place on a serving plate and garnish with lemon verbena sprigs and begonia blossoms.

SERVES 8

Top to bottom: Peach Brandy Pound Cake with Lemon Verbena,
Blueberry Crème Brûlée with Rose Geranium (recipe page 89)

4 cups (1 lb/500 g) strawberries, raspberries, blueberries and/or blackberries

1/4–1/2 cup (2–4 oz/60–125 g) granulated sugar, depending on the tartness of the berries

2 tablespoons berry liqueur (*optional*)

2 cups (10 oz/315 g) flour

2 1/2 teaspoons baking powder

1 teaspoon salt

1/4 cup (2 oz/60 g) granulated sugar

1/3 cup (3 oz/90 g) vegetable shortening (vegetable lard)

1/4 cup (1 oz/30 g) sliced (flaked) almonds, lightly toasted

3/4–1 cup (6–8 fl oz/180–250 ml) milk

1 cup (8 fl oz/250 ml) heavy (double) cream

1/3 cup (1 1/2 oz/45 g) sifted confectioners' (icing) sugar, plus sugar for dusting

2 tablespoons amaretto liqueur

SUMMER BERRY SHORTCAKE

Nothing provides a better finale to a summer barbecue than luscious shortcake topped with sweet, juicy berries and whipped cream. You can make the biscuits the day before, storing them at room temperature in an airtight container. The berries can be tossed with the sugar and, if you like, some berry liqueur up to several hours in advance.

Preheat an oven to 375°F (190°C). In large bowl, lightly toss the berries with the 1/4–1/2 cup (2–4 oz/60–125 g) granulated sugar and the berry liqueur, if using. Chill.

To make the shortcake, sift the flour, baking powder, salt and 1/4 cup (2 oz/60 g) granulated sugar into a medium bowl. Cut in the shortening with a pastry blender or 2 knives, then stir in the nuts. Lightly stir in as much milk as is needed to make a soft, moist dough. Turn the dough out onto a lightly floured work surface and lightly pat out 1/2 in (12 mm) thick. Using a biscuit cutter, cut the dough into six 2 1/2-in (6-cm) rounds. Place the biscuits, sides touching, on a baking sheet. Bake until they are lightly browned, 18–20 minutes. Let cool.

Right before serving, in a medium bowl, whip the cream until soft peaks form. Whisk in the 1/3 cup (1 1/2 oz/45 g) confectioners' sugar and amaretto liqueur, and a spoonful of berry juice, if desired. Split the biscuits in half crosswise.

On each of 6 large, chilled plates, place a split biscuit bottom, spoon the berries over it and top with a dollop of whipped cream. Place the biscuit top on slightly askew. Dust the rims of the plates with confectioners' sugar.

SERVES 6

1/2 cup (4 oz/125 g) unsalted
   butter, at room temperature

2 2/3 cups (22 oz/680 g) sugar

3 egg yolks plus 7 egg whites,
   at room temperature

3 cups (9 oz/280 g) sifted cake
   (soft-wheat) flour

1 tablespoon baking powder

3/4 teaspoon salt

1 1/3 cups (11 fl oz/335 ml) milk,
   at room temperature

1 tablespoon vanilla extract
   (essence)

3/4 teaspoon coconut extract
   (essence)

2/3 cup (5 fl oz/160 ml) water

1 teaspoon vanilla extract
   (essence)

1 cup (10 oz/315 g) prepared
   lemon curd or seedless
   raspberry preserves

3 cups (12 oz/375 g) sweetened,
   shredded coconut, toasted
   (see page 10)

COCONUT CAKE WITH
LEMON CURD FILLING

Pretty as can be, this classic coconut cake created by Ray L. Overton III, a food consultant from Atlanta, Georgia, is ideal for a springtime tea party, a baby or bridal shower or any festive occasion. Using ready-made lemon curd or raspberry preserves for the filling streamlines the preparation of the cake, which can be made the day before. If you prefer to make your own lemon curd, use the filling for Lemon-Raspberry Meringue Tart (see page 44).

Preheat an oven to 350°F (180°C). Lightly coat two 9-in (23-cm) round cake pans with vegetable cooking spray and dust with flour. To make the cake, in a large bowl, beat together the butter and 1 cup (8 oz/250 g) of the sugar until light and fluffy, about 3 minutes. Add the 3 egg yolks, one at a time, beating after each addition. In a medium bowl, sift together the flour, the baking powder and 1/2 teaspoon of the salt. Add the dry ingredients to the butter-sugar mixture alternately with the milk, beginning and ending with the flour. Beat in the 1 tablespoon vanilla and 1/2 teaspoon of the coconut extract.

In a large bowl, beat 3 of the egg whites until they form soft peaks. Gradually add 1/3 cup (3 oz/90 g) of the sugar while beating until glossy, stiff peaks form. Stir one-third of the beaten egg whites into the batter. Fold in the remaining beaten egg whites. Pour the batter into the prepared pans and bake until a toothpick inserted into the center comes out clean, 25–35 minutes. Cool the layers in the pans for 5 minutes, then remove from the pans and cool completely on a rack.

To make the icing, in a small, heavy saucepan over low heat, combine the remaining 1 1/3 cups (11 oz/340 g) sugar, the remaining 1/4 teaspoon of the salt and the water. Stir slowly until the sugar dissolves. Bring to a rolling boil. Cook the syrup until it reaches 230°F (110°C) on a candy thermometer. In a

large bowl, beat the remaining 4 egg whites until they form soft peaks. When the sugar syrup reaches 240°F (115°C), carefully pour into the egg whites in a slow, steady stream, beating constantly. Continue beating until cool, thick and glossy, about 7 minutes. Beat in the 1 teaspoon vanilla and the remaining $^1/_4$ teaspoon of the coconut extract.

Place one of the cake layers on a serving plate. Spread the top with lemon curd or raspberry preserves to within $^1/_2$ in (12 mm) from the edge. Top with the second layer. Spread the top and sides with a thick layer of icing. Carefully press the toasted coconut onto the top and sides of the cake. Refrigerate until ready to slice into wedges and serve.

SERVES 12–16

7 squares (7 oz/220 g) unsweetened chocolate

³/₄ cup (6 oz/185 g) unsalted butter

1¹/₂ cups (12 fl oz/375 ml) strong coffee

¹/₄ cup (2 fl oz/60 ml) bourbon

2 eggs

3 teaspoons vanilla extract (essence)

2 cups (8 oz/250 g) cake (soft-wheat) flour

1¹/₂ cups (12 oz/375 g) sugar

1 teaspoon baking soda (bicarbonate of soda)

¹/₄ teaspoon salt

2 cups (16 fl oz/500 ml) heavy (double) cream

fresh mint sprigs

EASY CHOCOLATE CAKE

According to one chocolate lover, this cake, which originated at the venerable Union Hotel in Benicia, California, is so good it can make you cry. Sliced thickly and served after a casual weeknight supper or weekend brunch, it requires no icing, just a spoonful of unsweetened whipped cream. The batter for the dark, rich, moist loaf is mixed quickly and easily with a spoon in a saucepan; you don't even need an electric mixer. The recipe yields two loaves; if you need only one, the extra one will freeze well—if you can resist temptation.

Preheat an oven to 275°F (135°C). Butter two 8¹/₂-by-4¹/₂-by-2¹/₂-in (22-by-11-by-6-cm) loaf pans and dust with flour.

Place the chocolate, butter and coffee in a heavy saucepan of about 4-qt (4-l) capacity. Set over low heat and stir almost constantly until the chocolate melts, then stir vigorously until the mixture is smooth and completely blended. Cool for about 10 minutes, then beat in the bourbon, eggs and 1 teaspoon of the vanilla. In a medium bowl, sift together the flour, sugar, baking soda and salt. Add to the chocolate mixture and beat until well blended and smooth. Divide the batter between the prepared pans and bake until a wooden toothpick inserted into the center of each loaf comes out clean, 45–55 minutes. Cool the cakes in the pans for 15 minutes, then turn out onto a rack to cool completely.

To make the topping, in a medium bowl, whip the cream and remaining 2 teaspoons vanilla until the cream barely stands in peaks. Cut the loaves into individual servings, arrange on plates and garnish with the whipped cream topping and fresh mint sprigs.

SERVES 16

2 cups (6 oz/180 g) sifted
(soft-wheat) cake flour

1³/₄ teaspoons baking powder

¹/₄ teaspoon ground nutmeg

³/₄ cup (6 fl oz/180 ml) half-
and-half (half cream), at room
temperature

·1 teaspoon vanilla extract (essence)

³/₄ cup (6 oz/185 g) unsalted butter,
at room temperature

1²/₃ cups (14 oz/430 g)
granulated sugar

2 eggs plus 2 egg whites and
3 egg yolks, at room temperature

¹/₄ cup (1 oz/30 g) sifted
all-purpose (plain) flour

1¹/₂ cups (12 fl oz/375 ml)
heavy (double) cream,
at room temperature

¹/₃ cup (3 fl oz/80 ml)
plus 1 tablespoon dry sherry

1¹/₄ cups (10 fl oz/310 ml)
heavy (double) cream, chilled

2 tablespoons confectioners'
(icing) sugar

15–20 candied rose petals

SHERRIED CREAM CAKE
WITH CANDIED ROSE PETALS

This showstopper of a white layer cake, developed by Atlanta food consultant Margaret Ann Surber, is perfect for a garden party. The cake and filling may be prepared the day before, but the cake must be assembled just before serving. You can find candied rose petals in the baking section of well-stocked markets.

Preheat an oven to 350°F (180°C). Lightly coat two 8-in (20-cm) round cake pans with vegetable cooking spray and dust with flour.

To make the cake, in a medium bowl, sift together the cake flour, baking powder and nutmeg. In a small bowl, whisk together the half-and-half and vanilla until well blended. In a large bowl, beat the butter and 1 cup (8 oz/250 g) of the granulated sugar until light and fluffy. Add the 2 eggs, one at a time, beating well after each addition. Beat in the flour mixture, alternating with the half-and-half mixture, in a total of 3 additions, ending with the flour. Beat after each addition until well blended.

In another large bowl, beat the 2 egg whites while adding ¹/₃ cup (3 oz/90 g) of the sugar in a slow, steady stream until well blended. Continue to beat until stiff, glossy peaks form. Stir about one-eighth of the beaten egg whites into the batter, then fold in the remaining egg whites until well blended.

Divide the batter between the prepared pans. Bake until a toothpick inserted into the centers comes out clean, 25–30 minutes. Cool the layers in the pans for 5 minutes, then remove from the pans and cool on a rack.

To make the custard, in a small, heavy nonreactive saucepan, whisk together the all-purpose flour, the remaining ¹/₃ cup (3 oz/90 g) of the granulated sugar and the 3 egg yolks until well blended. Slowly whisk in the 1¹/₂ cups (12 fl oz/375 ml) cream, then the ¹/₃ cup (3 oz/80 ml) sherry, until well blended and smooth. Set the saucepan over medium heat and cook, whisking constantly, until the mixture is very thick and begins to bubble, about 5 minutes. Remove from the heat and strain the custard through a fine-meshed sieve into a medium heatproof bowl. Cool to room temperature, then cover with

plastic wrap laid directly on the surface of the custard to prevent a skin from forming. Refrigerate at least 2 hours or for up to 24 hours before serving.

To make the topping, in a large bowl, beat the $1^1/_4$ cups (10 fl oz/310 ml) chilled cream until soft peaks form. Add the confectioners' sugar and 1 table-spoon sherry and continue to beat until stiff peaks form. Transfer to a fine-meshed sieve set in a bowl. Cover and refrigerate until ready to serve.

Place 1 cake layer on a cake pedestal. Spread the top evenly with two-thirds of the custard. Top with the second cake layer. Fold the remaining custard into the whipped cream mixture. Spread just enough of the topping on the top and sides of the cake, reserving the remainder to pipe decorations. Just before serving, using a #6 star tip, pipe a ring of rosettes around the top edge and base of the cake. Place the candied rose petals on alternating rosettes.

SERVES 10–12

PIES & TARTS

What dessert-making process could be simpler than to prepare a quick dough of flour, butter, sugar and water, roll it out, add fresh fruit and bake it? The results—a golden, flaky crust giving way to fragrant, juicy filling—far exceed the minimal effort.

The recipes in this chapter offer proof twelve times over that making a pie or tart for dessert is one of the surest ways to delight family and friends alike. Reveal a Blackberry Lattice Pie or an Apple Tart at the end of a casual supper, and everyone's eyes open wide with anticipated pleasure. Serve an Almond Tart at teatime, or replace a birthday cake with a Coffee-Toffee Pie lit by glowing candles, and guests know they're in for something truly special.

As these examples demonstrate, the world of pies and tarts offers a diversity of choices to suit every occasion or season. Sour Cream and Mixed Berry Tart can end a gala dinner party with understated elegance, while White Chocolate Banana Cream Pie has just the casual quality you'd want for a welcome-home supper. Key Lime Pie can cool the palate on a hot summer's day, while Caramel-Walnut Pie provides warmth on a cold winter's night.

Little will your guests realize that you've probably spent very little time in the kitchen preparing these festive creations. Easy as pie, indeed.

Bottom right: Key Lime Pie (recipe page 53)

1 cup (5 oz/155 g) flour

3/4 cup (6 oz/185 g) plus
   1 tablespoon sugar

1/4 teaspoon salt

1/4 teaspoon grated lemon zest

1/2 cup (4 oz/125 g) unsalted
   butter, chilled

1/2 teaspoon vanilla extract
   (essence)

1 tablespoon water, as needed

3/4 cup (6 fl oz/180 ml) heavy
   (double) cream

2 or 3 drops almond extract
   (essence)

1 teaspoon Grand Marnier liqueur

1 cup (4 oz/125 g) sliced
   (flaked) almonds

CHEZ PANISSE ALMOND TART

Through the years at the famous Berkeley restaurant, this tart has been one of the most popular desserts—thin and sweet, with a rich, chewy filling. The creation of dessert chef Lindsey Shere, it is almost foolproof. Serve it to conclude an elegant dinner party, garnished with whipped cream, if you like. You can make it up to a day before.

To make the tart pastry, in a medium bowl, combine the flour, the 1 tablespoon sugar, salt and lemon zest. Using a pastry blender or 2 knives, cut in the butter. Add the vanilla and, with your fingers, work the dough until it forms a ball. If it remains dry and will not form a ball, add the water. Pat into a small cake, wrap in plastic wrap and chill for about 30 minutes.

Preheat an oven to 425°F (220°C). On a lightly floured work surface, roll out the dough and fit it into a 9-in (23-cm) round or square tart pan. Trim the edges, prick the bottom evenly with a fork, line with aluminum foil and fill with pie weights or dried beans. Bake for 8 minutes, then remove the weights or beans and foil and bake until the shell appears dry but has not browned, about 4 minutes. Reduce the oven temperature to 400°F (200°C).

To make the filling, in a small saucepan over low heat, warm the cream and 3/4 cup (6 oz/185 g) sugar until the sugar has melted and the mixture is translucent. Blend in the almond extract and liqueur, then stir in the almonds. Pour the mixture into the tart shell, spreading it evenly.

Bake until the top is a deep golden brown, about 25 minutes. Cool in the pan, then gently ease the tart onto a serving plate. Serve at room temperature.

SERVES 8

1 cup (5 oz/155 g) flour

1/2 cup (4 oz/125 g) plus
   2 tablespoons sugar

pinch of salt

1/4 cup (2 oz/60 g) unsalted butter,
   at room temperature

1 egg, beaten

1 lb (500 g) pippin or
   Golden Delicious apples

1/4 cup (3 oz/90 g) honey,
   preferably thyme, rosemary
   or lavender

PROVENÇAL APPLE TART

Exemplary in its simplicity, this tart from southern France depends only upon the quality of the fruit and the pastry. Serve it at the end of a country-style dinner, or enjoy a slice with breakfast or afternoon coffee on a sunny terrace. The subtle flavor of the honey produced in the lavender fields of Provence (available at some specialty-food stores) lends an attractive nuance.

To make the tart pastry, in a medium bowl, combine the flour, 2 tablespoons sugar and salt. Make a well in the center of the dry ingredients and add the butter and egg. Stir and mash rapidly with a fork to form a coherent mass. Turn out onto a lightly floured work surface and knead briefly. Form the dough into a ball, wrap in plastic wrap and refrigerate for 2 hours.

Preheat an oven to 350°F (180°C). Butter a baking sheet. On a lightly floured work surface, roll out the pastry into a round about 1/8 in (3 mm) thick. Transfer it to the prepared baking sheet. Roll up and crimp the edges to shape a free-form circular tart shell with a rim 1/8–1/4 in (3–6 mm) high. Use a floured thumb or the back of the tines of a fork to form an attractive rim.

Halve and core the apples. Peel the halves, then cut each half crosswise into slices about 1/8 in (3 mm) thick. Arrange the slices in concentric circles starting just inside the pastry rim, overlapping the slices and the circles. Sprinkle with the 1/2 cup (4 oz/125 g) sugar. Bake until both the pastry and the apples are golden, 50–60 minutes.

Place the honey in a small bowl and immerse the base of the bowl in hot water for 2–3 minutes to make the honey more fluid. Remove the tart from the oven. Using a pastry brush, paint the apples with the honey. Slip the tart onto a platter and serve warm.

SERVES 8

1/2 cup (2 oz/60 g) ground walnuts
  (see page 14)

1³/4 cups (9 oz/280 g) flour

1 tablespoon ground cinnamon

2 tablespoons sugar

1/2 teaspoon salt

2/3 cup (5 oz/155 g) unsalted butter

1/3 cup (3 fl oz/80 ml) cold water

12 oz (375 g) cream cheese,
  at room temperature

1¹/3 cups (11 oz/340 g) plus
  3 tablespoons sugar

3 tablespoons flour

2 eggs

1¹/2 teaspoons vanilla extract
  (essence)

1 teaspoon grated lemon zest

4 cups (20 oz/625 g) diced
  fresh rhubarb

1/4 cup (2 fl oz/60 ml) water

RHUBARB CHEESECAKE TART

For those who appreciate bracing tartness to go with the sweetness of most desserts, this combination of cheesecake and fruit tart is superb. Serve it at the end of a dinner party or when you have friends over for coffee. It's a good idea to double the quantities when you make the walnut pastry dough and the rhubarb topping. Both freeze well, allowing you to enjoy the dessert at other times of year than spring and summer. Garnish with orange slices, if you like.

To make the tart pastry, in a medium bowl, combine the walnuts, the 1³/4 cups (9 oz/280 g) flour, the cinnamon, the 2 tablespoons sugar and the salt. Using a pastry blender or 2 knives, cut in the butter. Mix in the 1/3 cup (3 fl oz/80 ml) cold water until it is just combined. Shape the dough into a ball, flatten, wrap in plastic wrap and refrigerate for 1–1¹/2 hours.

Preheat an oven to 375°F (190°C). On a lightly floured work surface, roll out the dough and fit it into a 10-in (25-cm) round tart pan. Trim the edges, prick the bottom evenly with a fork, line with aluminum foil and fill with pie weights or dried beans. Bake until set but not browned, 15–20 minutes. Let cool and remove the weights or beans and foil.

To make the filling, in a medium bowl, beat the cream cheese, 3 tablespoons sugar, 3 tablespoons flour, eggs, vanilla and lemon zest until smooth, about 5–7 minutes. Fill the tart shell 1/4–1/2 in (6–12 mm) from the rim. Bake until the filling puffs a bit and is just firm to the touch, 20–25 minutes. Let cool.

To make the topping, in a medium saucepan over medium heat, combine the rhubarb, 1¹/3 cups (11 oz/340 g) sugar and 1/4 cup (2 fl oz/60 ml) water, bring to a boil and continue cooking until the rhubarb is tender and the liquid is reduced to a thick, syrupy compote, 10–12 minutes. Let cool.

Spread the rhubarb compote evenly over the cooled tart. Refrigerate until the topping is set, then ease the tart onto a serving plate. Serve cold or at room temperature.

SERVES 8

1 recipe tart pastry for
  Rhubarb Cheesecake Tart
  (see opposite page)

1 cup (8 fl oz/250 ml) milk

2 cups (1 lb/500 g) sugar

1 tablespoon vanilla extract
  (essence)

3 tablespoons cornstarch
  (cornflour)

1/4 teaspoon salt

4 egg yolks

1 cup (8 fl oz/250 ml) half-and-
  half (half cream)

2 cups (16 oz/500 ml)
  Pinot Noir wine

12 figs, halved

1 cup (4 oz/125 g) toasted and
  coarsely chopped walnuts
  (see page 14)

FRESH FIG TART
WITH WALNUTS

Plump and juicy, fresh figs are the ultimate summer fruit, traditionally enjoyed at the end of a casual lunch in the sun with crisp nuts and, perhaps, the last few sips of a glass of good red wine. Those three elements—figs, walnuts and red wine—are artfully combined in this easy tart.

Prepare the dough for the pastry crust and refrigerate.

To make the filling, in a heavy, medium saucepan over medium-low heat, combine the milk, 1 cup (8 oz/250 g) of the sugar, the vanilla, the cornstarch and the salt. Bring to a simmer and cook, stirring frequently, for 5 minutes. In a small bowl, beat together the egg yolks and half-and-half and gradually whisk into the milk-sugar mixture. Continue stirring until the pastry cream is smooth and thick. Remove from the heat and pour into a medium, cold bowl. Stir until it cools to room temperature, cover and refrigerate.

To make the topping, in a medium nonreactive saucepan over medium heat, combine the remaining 1 cup (8 oz/250 g) sugar and the Pinot Noir and bring to a simmer. Add the figs and poach until tender, 7–10 minutes. Remove the figs with a slotted spoon and set aside. Raise the heat to medium-high and cook the wine until reduced to a thick syrup, 20–25 minutes.

Preheat an oven to 375°F (190°C). On a lightly floured work surface, roll out the pastry to a 14-in (35-cm) circle and fit into a 10-in (25-cm) tart pan, allowing it to hang evenly over the edge. Tuck the edges of the dough down inside the rim of the pan, crimp the border and prick the bottom evenly with a fork. Line the pastry with aluminum foil, fill with pie weights or dried beans and bake until golden brown and crisp, 15–20 minutes. Let cool and remove the weights or beans and foil.

Pour the filling into the tart and smooth with a spatula. Arrange the poached fig halves on top of the cream and brush with the topping. Top with the toasted walnuts. Serve at room temperature.

SERVES 8

1 cup (5 oz/155 g) hazelnuts
(filberts), walnuts or almonds

3 tablespoons sugar

$^1/_4$ teaspoon ground nutmeg

$1^1/_2$ cups ($7^1/_2$ oz/235 g) flour

$^3/_4$ cup (6 oz/185 g) unsalted
butter

9 eggs

1 cup (8 oz/250 g) plus
6 tablespoons (3 oz/90 g) sugar

2 teaspoons grated lemon zest

pinch of salt

$^1/_2$ cup (4 oz/125 ml) lemon juice

$1^1/_2$ cups (6 oz/185 g) raspberries

$^1/_4$ teaspoon cream of tartar

LEMON-RASPBERRY
MERINGUE TART

Two giant steps beyond traditional lemon meringue pie, this dessert is ideal for a summer tea party or brunch. The tart shell may be baked, filled and refrigerated up to a day ahead. For an elegant presentation, individual tartlet pans may be used.

To make the tart pastry, place the nuts and sugar in a food processor fitted with the metal blade or in a blender and process until the nuts are finely chopped. In a medium bowl, combine the nut mixture, nutmeg and flour. With a pastry blender or 2 knives, cut in $^1/_2$ cup (4 oz/125 g) of the butter and then stir in 1 of the eggs. Stir until the mixture forms a dough. Cover and refrigerate for 20 minutes.

Preheat an oven to 350°F (180°C). Butter an 11-in (28-cm) tart pan. Press the dough evenly into the bottom and sides of the prepared pan. Trim the edges, prick the bottom evenly with a fork, line with aluminum foil and fill with pie weights or dried beans. Bake until golden, 25–30 minutes. Let cool and remove the weights or beans and foil.

To make the lemon filling, in a large bowl, place 4 of the eggs, 4 egg yolks, 1 cup (8 oz/250 g) of the sugar, the lemon zest, the salt and the lemon juice. Set the bowl over but not touching a pan of simmering water. Vigorously beat until the mixture has thickened, about 9 minutes. Beat in the remaining $^1/_4$ cup (2 oz/60 g) butter and remove from the heat. Do not overcook or it will curdle. Pour the lemon filling into the baked tart shell. Let cool to room temperature, then arrange the raspberries evenly on top of the filling.

Raise the oven temperature to 400°F (200°C). To make the meringue, in a medium bowl, beat the remaining 4 egg whites and the cream of tartar until frothy. Gradually beat in the remaining 6 tablespoons (3 oz/90 g) of sugar and continue beating until stiff, glossy peaks form. Pile the meringue onto the tart, sealing it onto the edge of the crust to keep the meringue from shrinking. Swirl the meringue decoratively with a spoon and bake until lightly browned, 8–10 minutes. Let cool. Serve at room temperature.

SERVES 8–10

1²/₃ cups (8 oz/250 g) flour, sifted

¹/₃ cup (2¹/₂ oz/75 g) superfine (castor) sugar

finely grated zest of 1 lemon

³/₄ cup (6 oz/185 g) unsalted butter, chilled, cut into small pieces

1–2 tablespoons ice water, as needed

7 egg yolks

²/₃ cup (4¹/₂ oz/145 g) superfine (castor) sugar

1 teaspoon vanilla extract (essence)

2 cups (1 lb/500 g) sour cream

2 cups (8 oz/250 g) mixed berries

SOUR CREAM AND MIXED BERRY TART

Use whichever spring, summer or autumn berries are plumpest, juiciest and most abundant for this tangy tart devised by chef Stephen Neale of Sydney, Australia. You can make it up to an evening ahead of time. If you wish, garnish with a rosette of mint leaves or a few fresh berries.

To make the tart pastry, in a large bowl, combine the flour, the ¹/₃ cup (2¹/₂ oz/75 g) superfine sugar and the lemon zest. Using a pastry blender or 2 knives, cut in the butter until the mixture is the consistency of rolled oats. Add 1 tablespoon of the water and mix with a fork until the dough feels damp and workable. Add the remaining 1 tablespoon water, if needed to achieve the proper consistency. Mix the dough until it comes together in a ball. Wrap in plastic wrap and refrigerate for 30 minutes.

Butter a deep 10-in (25-cm) tart pan. On a lightly floured work surface, roll out the dough and fit it into the prepared pan. Trim the edges, prick the bottom with a fork and refrigerate for 1 hour.

Preheat an oven to 350°F (180°C). Line the pastry with aluminum foil and fill with pie weights or dried beans. Bake until golden around the edges, 15–20 minutes. Remove the weights and foil and bake until the pastry is golden, 5 minutes longer. Let cool. Reduce the oven temperature to 300°F (150°C).

To make the filling, in a large bowl, whisk together the egg yolks and the ²/₃ cup (4¹/₂ oz/145 g) superfine sugar until pale, light and fluffy. Add the vanilla and sour cream and mix well.

Arrange the berries in the cooled tart shell. Pour the sour cream mixture evenly over the top. Bake until the mixture is firm but not set solidly, 20–30 minutes. Let cool, then cover and refrigerate for at least 3–4 hours or as long as overnight. To serve, ease the tart onto a serving plate and use a heated knife to cut into wedges.

SERVES 8

4 cups (1¹/₂ lb/750 g) black
  cherries (see recipe introduction)

2 eggs plus 1 egg yolk

¹/₂ cup (4 oz/125 g)
  granulated sugar

5 tablespoons (2¹/₂ oz/75 g)
  unsalted butter, melted

²/₃ cup (3 oz/90 g) flour

1 cup (8 fl oz/250 ml) milk

vanilla sugar (see page 17)

CLAFOUTIS

This almost cakelike baked custard from the Limousin region of France features ripe, juicy summer cherries. Traditionally, the cherries are not pitted, requiring you to warn your guests before they tuck into the dessert. Alternatively, you could pit them using a cherry pitter (available at kitchenware stores), which removes the pit without breaking too much of the skin or releasing excessive juice. Serve with Sunday brunch or dinner.

Preheat an oven to 400°F (200°C). Butter an ovenproof china or glazed earthenware mold large enough to hold the cherries in a single layer. Place the cherries in it.

In a medium bowl, combine the eggs and yolk. Add the granulated sugar and whisk until the mixture is pale in color. Whisk in the butter. Sift in the flour and mix well. Add the milk and continue beating until the batter is smooth. Pour over the cherries.

Bake until browned on top, about 40 minutes. Remove the clafoutis from the oven and sprinkle with vanilla sugar. Serve warm.

SERVES 6

1¼ cups (6½ oz/200 g) flour

1 cup (8 oz/250 g) plus
 ½ teaspoon sugar

¼ teaspoon salt

¼ cup (2 oz/60 g) unsalted butter,
 chilled

¼ cup (2 oz/60 g) vegetable
 shortening (vegetable lard),
 chilled

2 tablespoons cold water

2 cups (16 fl oz/500 ml) half-
 and-half (half cream)

⅓ cup (2 oz/60 g) flour

2 teaspoons butter

3 egg yolks, beaten

1 teaspoon vanilla extract
 (essence)

1 cup (4 oz/125 g) toasted walnuts
 (see page 14)

¼ teaspoon freshly grated nutmeg

CARAMEL-WALNUT PIE

Try this rich, crunchy, satisfying pie in place of or alongside pumpkin, mince-meat or apple on your holiday table. It's one of the best uses for a bumper crop of walnuts. You could also try it with pecans or hazelnuts. For a pretty decoration, cut scraps of the pastry dough into leaves to place atop the filling. Serve with whipped cream.

To make the pie pastry, in a medium bowl, combine the 1¼ cups (6½ oz/ 200 g) flour, ½ teaspoon sugar and salt. Using a pastry blender or 2 knives, cut in the ¼ cup (2 oz/60 g) unsalted butter and the vegetable shortening until the mixture resembles coarse crumbs. Add the water, 1 tablespoon at a time, and mix gently with a fork to form a soft dough. Wrap in plastic wrap and chill for 1 hour.

On a lightly floured work surface, roll out the pastry. Fit into a 9-in (23-cm) pie pan and trim the edges. Refrigerate until using.

To make the filling, in a large, heavy saucepan, caramelize the 1 cup (8 oz/ 250 g) sugar by stirring it over high heat until the sugar turns golden brown, about 10 minutes; take care not to burn it. Remove the sugar from the heat immediately, as it will continue to cook. In a small saucepan over medium heat, bring the half-and-half to a low boil. Warm the caramelized sugar over low heat and gradually stir the hot half-and-half into it. If the caramel balls up in the cream, continue stirring until it melts into the sauce. Remove from the heat and let cool to room temperature, about 30 minutes.

Preheat an oven to 375°F (190°C). Whisk the ⅓ cup (2 oz/60 g) flour, 2 tea-spoons butter, egg yolks and vanilla into the caramel. Stir in the walnuts. Sprinkle the nutmeg over the pastry shell, pour in the filling and bake for 10 minutes. Reduce the heat to 325°F (165°C) and bake until a toothpick inserted into the center comes out clean, 30 minutes longer. Serve warm.

SERVES 8

1 cup (5 oz/155 g) flour

1 cup (8 oz/250 g) unsalted butter, softened

1/4 cup (2 oz/60 g) firmly packed brown sugar

1 oz (30 g) unsweetened chocolate, grated

1 teaspoon vanilla extract (essence)

2 tablespoons milk, or more as needed

3/4 cup (3 oz/90 g) finely chopped walnuts

3/4 cup (6 oz/185 g) granulated sugar

1 1/2 tablespoons plus 2 teaspoons powdered instant coffee

1 oz (30 g) unsweetened chocolate, melted

2 eggs

1 1/2 cups (12 fl oz/375 ml) heavy (double) cream, chilled

1/2 cup (2 oz/60 g) confectioners' (icing) sugar

1 1/2 tablespoons nonfat dry milk (milk powder)

1 tablespoon grated unsweetened chocolate

BLUM'S COFFEE-TOFFEE PIE

Patrons of the late, lamented Blum's restaurant in San Francisco referred to this irresistible dessert as a candy bar masquerading as a pie. Serve it when your guest of honor has a real sweet tooth, or any time you feel the need to indulge or be indulged. You will need an electric mixer for the long beating of the filling and a couple of hours for the pie to chill before it is served. For a really special presentation, garnish with chocolate leaves, available at chocolatiers or fine pastry shops. (photograph page 8)

Preheat an oven to 375°F (190°C). To make the pastry, in a medium bowl, combine the flour, 1/2 cup (4 oz/125 g) of the butter, the brown sugar and the 1 oz (30 g) grated chocolate. Using your fingertips or a pastry blender, mix until well blended. Add the vanilla, 2 tablespoons milk and walnuts. Stir until the mixture forms a cohesive mass. If it is too dry, add a few drops more milk.

Form the cookielike dough into walnut-sized pieces and press onto the bottom and sides of a 9-in (23-cm) pie pan, distributing them evenly, with no gaps or thin spots. Crimp the edges, prick the pastry evenly with a fork, line with aluminum foil and fill with pie weights or dried beans. Bake for 8 minutes, remove the weights or beans and foil and bake until the shell is dry and crisp, about 10 minutes more. Let cool.

To make the filling, in a large bowl, beat the remaining 1/2 cup (4 oz/125 g) butter until fluffy. Continue to beat, gradually adding the granulated sugar. Beat in the 2 teaspoons instant coffee and the melted chocolate. Add 1 egg and beat for 5 minutes. Add the second egg and beat for 5 minutes more. Spread the filling evenly in the cooled pie shell, then cover and refrigerate for at least 6 hours or as long as overnight.

To prepare the topping, in a large bowl, combine the cream, confectioners' sugar, dry milk and 1 1/2 tablespoons instant coffee and beat until stiff peaks are formed. Spread in peaks and swirls over the chilled pie and sprinkle with the grated chocolate. Refrigerate for at least 2 hours before serving.

SERVES 8

1 recipe tart pastry for
  Sour Cream and Mixed Berry
  Tart (see page 47)

1 lb (500 g) cream cheese,
  at room temperature

3$^{1}/_{2}$ cups (28 fl oz/875 ml) low-fat
  sweetened condensed milk

$^{3}/_{4}$ cup (6 fl oz/180 ml) Key lime
  juice (10–15 Key limes)

1 teaspoon grated Key lime zest

$^{1}/_{4}$ teaspoon salt

2 cups (16 fl oz/500 ml) heavy
  (double) cream, chilled

1 teaspoon vanilla extract (essence)

3 tablespoons confectioners'
  (icing) sugar

KEY LIME PIE

Authentic Key lime pie does not look lime green. It's pale yellow, from the tangy juice of the limes grown on the Florida Keys since the 1830s. Today, most recipes call for a graham cracker crust, but original versions used a pastry shell, which does not overpower the delicate filling. If you like, garnish with strips of Key lime zest. (photograph pages 36–37)

Prepare the dough for the pastry crust and refrigerate for 30 minutes. Butter a deep 9-in (23-cm) pie pan. On a lightly floured work surface, roll out the dough and fit it into the prepared pan. Trim the edges, prick the bottom evenly with a fork and refrigerate for 1 hour.

Preheat an oven to 350°F (180°C). Line the pastry with aluminum foil and fill with pie weights or dried beans. Bake until golden around the edges, 15–20 minutes. Remove the weights and foil and bake until the pastry is golden, about 5 minutes longer. Let cool.

To make the filling, in a large bowl, beat the cream cheese and condensed milk until well blended and smooth. Beat in the lime juice, lime zest and salt until well blended. Spoon into the pie shell, smoothing the surface. Cover and refrigerate until completely chilled and set, about 3 hours.

To make the topping, in a medium bowl, beat the cream and vanilla until soft peaks form. Add the confectioners' sugar and continue to beat until stiff peaks form. Transfer the whipped cream mixture to a fine-mesh sieve set over a bowl to catch any liquid. Cover tightly with plastic wrap and refrigerate for up to 2 hours.

To serve, spread the topping evenly over the chilled pie. Swirl and peak the whipped cream for a decorative touch.

SERVES 8

SORBETS, ICE CREAMS & COOKIES

In recent years, fashionable restaurants everywhere have enthusiastically taken to adding ice cream and cookies to their dessert menus. These might well be served with the high style you'd expect from a pricey establishment—scoops of three to five different flavors arranged in a starburst pattern on a chilled china plate, with the cookies nestled in a starched linen napkin. When you get right down to it, the dessert's appeal is anything but haute. Instead, it reaches back to childhood and fondly remembered summertime treats.

Such is the elemental power frozen desserts and cookies have to please us. Each on its own can make any gathering feel more festive: stately Ice Cream Plombières to end a sophisticated meal or delicate Lace Cookies to complement the finery of a tea or shower. And no matter how impressive the effect, they provide the host or hostess with the added benefit of easy preparation.

Served together, frozen desserts and cookies offer a prime example of culinary synergy, where the whole effect far exceeds the sum of the two parts. Consider this chapter's dynamic pairings of Blackberry Cassis Sorbet with Rosemary Cookies and Red Grapefruit–Champagne Sorbet with Tortilla Cinnamon Crisps. Drawing from your glimmering childhood memories, you can use the recipes here to come up with countless creative combinations of your own.

Outside to inside: Stuffed Butter Cookies (recipe page 65), Almond Cookies (recipe page 68)

59

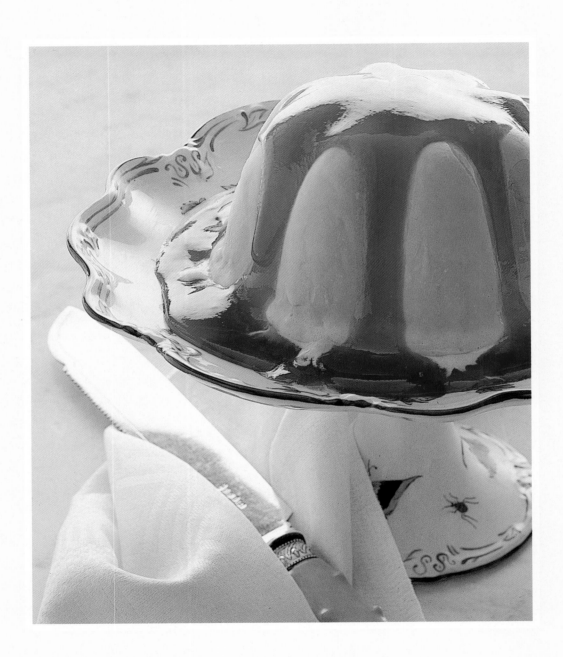

6 cups (48 fl oz/1.5 l) heavy
(double) cream

1¹/₃ cups (7 oz/220 g) blanched
almonds

1 cup (8 fl oz/250 ml) milk

10 egg yolks

1 cup (8 oz/250 g) sugar

¹/₂ teaspoon almond extract
(essence)

³/₄ cup (6 oz/185 g) apricot jam

ICE CREAM PLOMBIÈRES

To honor Napoleon III's visit to the resort town of Plombières-les-Bains in 1858, the keeper of a local eating house invented this jam-coated ice cream confection. You can prepare the ice cream and freeze it up to several days ahead of time, making this an easy-yet-impressive warm-weather dessert for any party at which you wish to treat your guests like special dignitaries.

In a large saucepan over medium heat, bring 4 cups (32 fl oz/1 l) of the cream to a boil. Transfer to a food processor fitted with the metal blade or to a blender. Add the almonds and milk and process until the almonds are ground, then pour the mixture through a strainer back into the saucepan.

In a large saucepan, combine the egg yolks and sugar and whisk until the mixture is very pale in color. Add the almond-cream mixture and cook over low heat, stirring constantly, until the custard coats a spoon. Remove from the heat and add the almond extract. Let cool, stirring from time to time.

In a medium bowl, whip the remaining 2 cups (16 fl oz/500 ml) cream until soft peaks are formed. Fold into the custard. Pour into a large round or square mold with an 8-cup (64–fl oz/2-l) capacity and freeze until firm, 4–6 hours.

In a small saucepan over low heat, warm the jam. Force through a fine-mesh sieve and let cool.

To serve, plunge the mold into hot water for 20 seconds, then unmold the ice cream onto a serving plate. Coat with the jam and spoon on individual plates.

SERVES 8

RED GRAPEFRUIT– CHAMPAGNE SORBET WITH TORTILLA CINNAMON CRISPS

5 cups (40 fl oz/1.25 l) freshly
squeezed red grapefruit juice

1¹/₂ cups (12 oz/375 g) sugar

¹/₄ cup (2 fl oz/60 ml) light
corn syrup

1 tablespoon finely grated
grapefruit zest

³/₄ cup (6 fl oz/180 ml) Champagne
or pink sparkling wine

4 flour tortillas

vegetable oil, for deep-frying

1 tablespoon ground cinnamon

1 teaspoon ground cloves

candied citrus peel

To make this sorbet, which literally sparkles on the palate, look for ruby red grapefruit in well-stocked supermarkets. You can also use pink ones, or even regular grapefruit, though the color will not compare. You can also freeze the sorbet in shallow freezer trays, stirring the mixture every hour until solid; this will yield a more granular consistency. The spicy-sweet tortilla triangles, which make a delicious accompaniment, can be made up to 2 days ahead and stored in an airtight container at room temperature.

To make the sorbet, in a large saucepan over medium heat, combine the grapefruit juice, 1¹/₄ cups (10 oz/315 g) of the sugar, the corn syrup and the grapefruit zest. Cook, stirring constantly, until the sugar dissolves. Strain through a fine-mesh sieve into a large bowl, then stir in the Champagne or sparkling wine. Cover and chill well. Transfer to an ice cream maker and freeze according to the manufacturer's instructions.

To make the crisps, cut each tortilla into 8 triangles. In a deep sauté pan over high heat, pour in oil to a depth of 1 in (2.5 cm). Heat to 360°F (182°C) on a deep-fat thermometer. Working in batches, add the triangles to the hot oil and fry, turning once, until crisp and golden, 2–3 minutes total. Drain on paper towels. In a small bowl, stir together the cinnamon, cloves and remaining ¹/₄ cup (2 oz/60 g) sugar and sprinkle over the triangles while still warm.

To serve, scoop the sorbet into small chilled bowls. Garnish with the tortilla crisps and the candied citrus peel.

SERVES 8–10

Clockwise from left: Blackberry Cassis Sorbet with Rosemary Cookies (recipe page 64), Red Grapefruit–Champagne Sorbet with Tortilla Cinnamon Crisps

1 cup (5 oz/155 g) flour

1/2 cup (4 oz/125 g) unsalted
butter, at room temperature

1 1/4 cups (10 oz/310 g)
granulated sugar

1 egg yolk, beaten

1/2 teaspoon vanilla extract
(essence)

2 tablespoons chopped fresh
rosemary leaves

1 3/4 teaspoons finely grated
lemon zest

pinch of salt

confectioners' (icing) sugar

4 cups (1 lb/500 g) blackberries

1 1/4 cups (10 fl oz/310 ml)
plus 6 tablespoons
(3 fl oz/90 ml) water

2 teaspoons lime juice

crème de cassis or blackberry-
flavored liqueur

lavender flowers (see page 13)
and fresh rosemary sprigs

BLACKBERRY CASSIS SORBET WITH ROSEMARY COOKIES

The vibrant purple sorbet, partnered with herb-scented butter cookies, enlivens the taste buds after a dinner party featuring spicy foods. Both can be made 1 week in advance (store the cookies in an airtight container at room temperature). (photograph page 63)

To make the cookies, in a medium bowl, place the flour. Using a pastry blender or 2 knives, cut in the butter until the mixture resembles coarse crumbs. Add 1/2 cup (4 oz/125 g) of the sugar, mixing well. Add the egg yolk, vanilla, rosemary leaves, lemon zest and salt and stir until the mixture forms a dough. Gather into a ball and divide in half. On a lightly floured work surface, roll each portion into a log 2 in (5 cm) in diameter. Wrap each log in plastic wrap and refrigerate for 2–3 hours. Preheat an oven to 350°F (180°C). Cut each log crosswise into slices 1/4 in (6 mm) thick and arrange on 2 ungreased baking sheets. Sprinkle with confectioners' sugar. Bake until light brown around the edges, about 10 minutes. Transfer to a rack to cool.

To make the sorbet, in a large saucepan over medium-high heat, combine the blackberries and the 6 tablespoons (3 fl oz/90 ml) water. Cover and simmer until soft, 10 minutes. Uncover, raise the heat to high and cook until thickened, 6–8 minutes. Place in a blender or in a food processor fitted with a metal blade and purée until smooth, then pass through a fine-mesh sieve into a large measuring cup. In a small saucepan over high heat, combine the remaining 3/4 cup (6 oz/185 g) sugar and the 1 1/4 cups (10 fl oz/310 ml) water. Bring to a boil, stirring to dissolve the sugar. Boil until syrupy, about 10 minutes. Let cool slightly, then stir in the lime juice. Add the syrup to the blackberries, then add enough water to measure 3 cups (24 fl oz/750 ml) total. Pour into a shallow metal pan and freeze until firm, about 3 hours. Remove and process in the blender or food processor until smooth. Refreeze and repeat.

To serve, spoon the sorbet into chilled wineglasses and drizzle with crème de cassis or blackberry liqueur. Top with the lavender flowers. Arrange the cookies in a napkin-lined basket and tuck in a few rosemary sprigs.

SERVES 6

FOR THE DATE FILLING:

1 lb (500 g) pitted dates, chopped

¹/₂ cup (4 fl oz/125 ml) water

finely grated zest of 1 orange

¹/₂ teaspoon ground cinnamon

FOR THE NUT FILLING:

2 cups (8 oz/250 g) chopped
   walnuts, almonds or pistachios

1 cup (8 oz/250 g) granulated sugar

1 tablespoon rosewater

2 teaspoons ground cinnamon

FOR THE PASTRY:

1 cup (8 oz/250 g) unsalted
   butter, at room temperature

2 tablespoons granulated sugar

2 cups (8 oz/250 g) sifted flour

2–4 tablespoons milk

1 tablespoon rosewater or
   orangeflower water

confectioners' (icing) sugar

STUFFED BUTTER COOKIES

Choose whichever filling—date or nut—most appeals to you for these traditional Syrian Easter cookies, a great treat for a spring holiday celebration. They are easy to prepare, once you get a feel for the way the dough is folded around the filling. Store them in an airtight container at room temperature for up to 1 week. (photograph pages 58–59)

Choose either the date or the nut filling. To make the date filling, in a medium saucepan over medium heat, combine the dates and water and bring to a boil. Reduce the heat to low and simmer, stirring occasionally, until the dates form a paste, about 5 minutes. Stir in the orange zest and cinnamon. To make the nut filling, in a large bowl, stir together the nuts, granulated sugar, rosewater and ground cinnamon.

Preheat an oven to 300°F (150°C). To make the cookie pastry, in a large bowl, beat together the butter and granulated sugar until light and fluffy. Beat in the flour and then the milk and flower water. Knead in the bowl until the dough holds together and is easy to shape.

Pinch off a walnut-sized piece of dough. Roll it between your palms into a ball and hollow it out with your thumb. Pinch the sides up to form a pot shape. Place a spoonful of filling into the hollow, then pinch the dough closed over the filling. Press and then score the sealed edge, if desired.

Place the filled balls on an ungreased baking sheet. Bake until firm and fully set, about 20 minutes; do not brown. Transfer the cookies to racks. Sprinkle generously with confectioners' sugar while still warm, then cool completely and serve.

MAKES ABOUT 2¹/₂ DOZEN COOKIES

1 qt (1 l) vanilla ice cream,
   softened at room temperature
   for about 30 minutes

2–3 teaspoons rosewater,
   or more as needed

4 cups (1½ lb/750 g) semisweet
   (plain) chocolate chips

2 tablespoons vegetable oil

rose petals, baby rosebuds,
   miniature roses or candied violets
   (see page 13)

ROSE-SCENTED ICE CREAM
IN CHOCOLATE SEASHELLS

A little imagination can transform store-bought ice cream into a lovely dessert—perhaps to conclude a romantic dinner. You'll find rosewater in the baking section of well-stocked supermarkets and the scallop shells used to form the chocolate in crafts stores. The chocolate shells can be refrigerated for up to 3 days.

Place the ice cream in a large bowl and beat in rosewater to taste, starting with 2–3 teaspoons. The ice cream should be delicately flavored, not overwhelming. Repack the ice cream into its container and refreeze.

To make the chocolate seashells, cover the inside of six to eight 4- to 5-in (10- to 13-cm) scallop shells tightly with aluminum foil. In the top pan of a double boiler over gently simmering water, melt the chocolate chips with the vegetable oil. Let cool slightly. Using a flat brush, spread the chocolate evenly over the foil, forming a smooth, thick coating. Place on waxed paper–lined baking sheets and chill until firm, 30–45 minutes. Carefully remove the chocolate shells, then peel away the foil. Reheat the remaining chocolate and use to repair any cracks and to paint the inside of each chocolate shell.

To serve, scoop the ice cream into the shells. Garnish with the flowers.

SERVES 6–8

8 egg yolks

2 cups (1 lb/500 g) sugar

3 cups (24 fl oz/750 ml) milk

2 cups (16 fl oz/500 ml) heavy
(double) cream

3–4 tablespoons lemon juice,
depending on the tartness of
the fruit

6 nectarines, peeled (see page 13),
pitted and diced

nectarine slices

FRESH NECTARINE ICE CREAM

After a summer barbecue, what could be better than homemade ice cream? You can use peaches, plums or berries in place of the nectarines.

In a large bowl, beat the egg yolks until pale and thick. Gradually beat in 1 cup (8 oz/250 g) of the sugar, then beat in the milk and the cream. Transfer the mixture to a large saucepan and cook over low heat, stirring constantly, until slightly thickened, 7–10 minutes. Pour into a large bowl and let cool to room temperature, stirring frequently. Place in the freezer until partially frozen, 3–5 hours. Stir every 30 minutes to prevent ice crystals from forming, or partially freeze in an ice cream maker according to the manufacturer's instructions.

To make the compote, in a medium, nonreactive saucepan, heat the remaining 1 cup (8 oz/250 g) sugar and lemon juice over low heat. When the sugar dissolves and the mixture begins to boil, add the nectarines and simmer until tender, 4–6 minutes. Cover and chill completely in the refrigerator. Mix the compote thoroughly into the partially frozen ice cream. Let the ice cream freeze to the desired texture, continuing to stir every 30 minutes. To finish freezing in an ice cream maker, follow the manufacturer's instructions. To serve, scoop into small chilled bowls and garnish with nectarine slices.

SERVES 6–8

3 cups (1¹/₄ lb/625 g) blanched
  almonds, finely ground
  (see page 14)

1¹/₄ cups (10 oz/310 g)
  granulated sugar

1 tablespoon finely grated
  lemon zest

2 eggs

1 cup (8 fl oz/250 ml) water

1 tablespoon orangeflower water

2 cups (8 oz/250 g) confectioners'
  (icing) sugar

ALMOND COOKIES

This recipe, originating in Algeria, makes a fitting conclusion to any Mediterranean or Far Eastern meal. Try serving the sweet, chewy cookies with strong coffee in the morning or with mint tea in the afternoon. They can be made 1 week ahead of time and kept in an airtight container at room temperature. You'll find orangeflower water in Middle Eastern shops and well-stocked supermarkets. (photograph pages 58–59)

Preheat an oven to 350°F (180°C). Line 2 large baking sheets with parchment paper or leave ungreased.

In a large bowl, combine the almonds, 1 cup (8 oz/250 g) of the granulated sugar and the lemon zest and stir to mix. Make a well in the center and add the eggs. Gradually mix until a smooth dough forms.

Divide the dough in half. On a generously floured work surface, roll each half into a log 18 in (45 cm) long and 1¹/₂ in (4 cm) in diameter. Flatten the log into an oblong 1¹/₂ in (4 cm) thick and 2 in (5 cm) wide. Cut on the diagonal into slices 1 in (2.5 cm) thick. Dust the slices with flour and place on the prepared baking sheets 1 in (2.5 cm) apart. Bake until pale gold, about 15 minutes. Transfer to racks to cool.

In a medium saucepan over high heat, combine the remaining ¹/₄ cup (2 oz/60 g) granulated sugar and the water. Bring to a boil, stirring until the sugar dissolves. Cook over high heat until a thin syrup forms. Pour into a shallow bowl and let cool. Stir the orangeflower water into the cooled syrup.

Spread the confectioners' sugar in a shallow pan. Dip the cooled cookies first in the syrup and then in the sugar. Set on a rack to dry, then serve.

MAKES 2 DOZEN COOKIES

¹/₃ cup (3 oz/90 g) unsalted butter,
   at room temperature

1¹/₂ tablespoons granulated sugar

1 egg, at room temperature

¹/₃ cup (3 fl oz/80 ml)
   sorghum syrup

2 teaspoons low-fat buttermilk,
   at room temperature

2¹/₄ cups (9 oz/280 g) sifted flour

¹/₂ teaspoon baking soda
   (bicarbonate of soda)

1 teaspoon ground cinnamon

granulated sugar or confectioners'
   (icing) sugar

SORGHUM TEA COOKIES

These cookies, from Margaret Agnew's Southern Traditions, *are small and dainty, with a light caramel color that comes from sorghum syrup, available in most well-stocked supermarkets, gourmet shops and health-food stores. After refrigerating the dough overnight, you can cut them out with cookie cutters, then decorate them after cooling with a light dusting of confectioners' sugar, and you have a perfect ending to a luncheon or bridge club social. The cookies keep for up to 2 weeks stored in an airtight container. If you don't want to bake them all at once, you can wrap the dough tightly in plastic wrap and refrigerate for up to 2 days. (photograph page 71)*

In a large bowl, cream the butter. Gradually add the granulated sugar, beating until light and fluffy. Add the egg and beat well. Add the sorghum syrup and buttermilk. Mix well.

In a large bowl, sift together the flour, baking soda and cinnamon. Gradually add the flour mixture to the butter mixture and stir until well blended. The dough will be sticky and elastic. Wrap the dough in plastic wrap and refrigerate overnight.

Preheat an oven to 375°F (190°C). Lightly coat a baking sheet with vegetable cooking spray. On a generously floured work surface, roll out the dough ¹/₄ in (6 mm) thick. The dough will be very sticky; sprinkle lightly with flour, as needed, to prevent sticking. Using a 1¹/₂-in (4-cm) round cookie cutter, cut out the cookies, flouring the cutter between cuts. Place on the prepared baking sheet about ¹/₄ in (6 mm) apart. Sprinkle lightly with granulated sugar. Alternatively, after the cookies are baked and cooled, using a fine-mesh sieve, dust with confectioners' sugar.

Bake until crisp and golden brown, 8–10 minutes. Transfer to racks to cool, then serve.

MAKES ABOUT 3 DOZEN COOKIES

3 oz (90 g) cream cheese,
   at room temperature

$^1/_2$ cup (4 oz/125 g) unsalted
   butter, at room temperature

1 cup (4 oz/125 g) sifted flour

1 egg, at room temperature

$^2/_3$ cup (5 oz/155 g) firmly packed
   dark brown sugar

2 tablespoons unsalted butter,
   melted

1 teaspoon vanilla extract
   (essence)

$^1/_2$ teaspoon salt

$^3/_4$ cup (3 oz/90 g) coarsely
   chopped pecans

PECAN TASSIES

Tassies, Lilliputian tartlets with a cream cheese crust, are much enjoyed by South-erners, who fill these two-bite-sized morsels with a mixture much like pecan pie. According to Nathalie Dupree in her book New Southern Cooking, *tassies are "frequently served at weddings and special occasions which may require a finger-food dessert treat." Such occasions often require treats in large quantity, and tassies have the added advantage of freezing well for up to 1 month.*

To make the pastry, in a food processor fitted with the dough blade, combine the cream cheese and the $^1/_2$ cup (4 oz/125 g) butter. Add the flour and pulse until well blended and a soft dough forms. Wrap the dough in plastic wrap and refrigerate for $1^1/_2$ hours.

Shape the dough into 24 balls, using about 2 teaspoons of the dough for each. Wrap the balls in plastic wrap and refrigerate for 30 minutes.

Preheat an oven to 350°F (180°C). Lightly coat 2 miniature muffin pans with vegetable cooking spray. Place the dough balls in the prepared muffin cups and press against the bottom and sides to form shells. Place the pans of pastry shells in a freezer while you prepare the filling.

In a medium bowl, combine the egg, brown sugar, 2 tablespoons melted butter, vanilla and salt and stir until well blended and smooth. Stir in the pecans. Fill each shell with 2 teaspoons of filling. Bake until a toothpick inserted into the center comes out clean and the crusts are golden brown, 20–25 minutes. Cool the tartlets in the pans for 5 minutes, then transfer to racks to cool completely. Serve at room temperature.

MAKES 2 DOZEN TASSIES

Clockwise from top: Pecan Tassies, Southern Lace Cookies (recipe page 75), Sorghum Tea Cookies (recipe page 69)

Top to bottom: Cream Horns, Madeleines (recipe page 74)

¹/₄ cup (2 oz/60 g) unsalted butter

2 egg whites

³/₄ cup (5 oz/155 g) superfine (castor) sugar

¹/₂ cup (2¹/₂ oz/75 g) flour

1 tablespoon dark rum

2¹/₂ cups (20 fl oz/625 ml) very cold heavy (double) cream

2 teaspoons vanilla sugar (see page 17) or ¹/₄ teaspoon vanilla extract (essence)

CREAM HORNS

Resembling miniature ice cream cones, these delightful little cream-filled pastries are certain to attract comment at a tea party. The horns themselves can be prepared several hours in advance, but should be served the moment they have been filled with the whipped cream.

Preheat an oven to 375°F (190°C). Butter 2 baking sheets. In a small saucepan over low heat, melt the butter. Let cool. In a medium bowl, beat the egg whites until frothy. Mix in the sugar. Sift in the flour and stir to combine. Beat in the melted butter and the rum.

Drop the batter by tablespoons onto the baking sheets; it will spread out slightly to form small circles. Bake until the pastry circles are just golden, 8–10 minutes. Quickly form the hot wafers into cone shapes. Insert the point of each pastry cone into the neck of a bottle to hold its shape until it cools.

In a medium bowl, whip the cream and vanilla sugar or vanilla extract until soft peaks form. Spoon into a pastry bag filled with a small fluted tip and pipe into the cones. Serve immediately.

SERVES 6

3 eggs

$^1/_4$ cup ($1^1/_2$ oz/45 g) superfine
(castor) sugar

$^1/_2$ teaspoon orangeflower water

$^1/_4$ cup (2 oz/60 g) unsalted butter,
at room temperature

$^1/_2$ cup ($2^1/_2$ oz/75 g) flour

vanilla sugar (see page 17)

MADELEINES

These delicate yet rich-tasting shell-shaped sponge cookies are the very stuff that, with just one bite, sent Marcel Proust's imagination off on his Remembrance of Things Past. *There's no telling what flights of fancy they'll spark at an afternoon tea. To bake them, you'll need a special madeleine tin, sold in well-stocked kitchenware stores. The madeleines keep well in an airtight container at room temperature for up to 1 week. (photograph page 72)*

Preheat an oven to 375°F (190°C). Butter 20–24 madeleine molds, depending on their size.

In a medium bowl, combine the eggs and superfine sugar and beat until pale in color. Add the orangeflower water and butter and stir to combine. Sift in the flour and fold in gently.

Divide the batter among the molds, filling them three-fourths full. Bake until the madeleines have risen and are lightly browned, about 15 minutes. Cool on a rack, sprinkle with vanilla sugar and serve.

MAKES ABOUT 2 DOZEN MADELEINES

1 cup (4 oz/125 g) pecans, toasted
and finely chopped (see page 14)

1 cup (4 oz/125 g) sifted flour

$^1/_4$ cup (2 oz/60 g) granulated sugar

$^1/_4$ cup (2 oz/60 g) firmly packed
light brown sugar

$^1/_2$ teaspoon salt

$^1/_4$ cup (2 fl oz/60 ml) light
corn syrup

$^1/_2$ cup (4 oz/125 g) unsalted butter

$^1/_2$ teaspoon vanilla extract
(essence)

SOUTHERN LACE COOKIES

These thin, ethereal cookies have a texture that resembles lace, with the added crunch of pecans. Some recipes include oatmeal for a coarser texture. This extremely delicious version is more refined and dainty, the perfect treat for a shower or tea. Make them up to 4 days ahead and store between layers of waxed paper in an airtight container or up to 1 month ahead and freeze. (photograph page 71)

Preheat an oven to 350°F (180°C). Line 2 baking sheets with aluminum foil, placing the shiny side of the foil face down, and butter lightly.

In a large bowl, combine the pecans and flour. In a large, heavy saucepan over medium-low heat, combine the granulated sugar, brown sugar, salt, corn syrup and butter. Cook, stirring constantly, until the butter has melted and sugars have dissolved, about 5 minutes. Remove from the heat. Gradually add the flour-pecan mixture, stirring until well blended. Stir in the vanilla.

Drop the batter by tablespoonfuls onto the lined baking sheets, allowing only 6 cookies per baking sheet and leaving at least 3 in (7.5 cm) between the cookies. Press each cookie flat and even, to a diameter of about 3 in (7.5 cm).

Bake until golden brown and bubbly, 8–10 minutes. Keeping the cookies on the aluminum foil, transfer the foil to racks to cool for 2–3 minutes. When the cookies are firm but still warm, remove the foil and return the cookies to the racks to cool completely. If the cookies become too firm to remove from the foil, place in the oven briefly to soften. Serve at room temperature.

MAKES ABOUT 2 DOZEN COOKIES

GRAND FINALES

Some desserts defy neat description. Is Pavlova a meringue, a mousse, a pudding or a fruit tart? Yes on all counts. Or how about the Bananas Foster from New Orleans' legendary Brennan's restaurant? Calling it an ice cream dessert would be selling it short. Saying that it features flambéed fruit does not begin to touch upon its diverse glories.

The eleven recipes that follow share the common bond that they cannot be easily categorized. The resistance to labeling stems from the fact that most of these desserts are composed of several different elements—the zabaglione, coffee-flavored mascarpone cheese and ladyfingers layered to make a classic Italian Tiramisù, for example, or the fresh fruit, scented custard cream and crisp caramel topping of Blueberry Crème Brûlée with Rose Geranium.

As the descriptions suggest, such desserts might take a little more time or work than others in this book. This does not necessarily mean that they are difficult. If you reduce each recipe down to its basic elements, the steps become simple; and much of the work can be done well in advance, with the final assembly left until just before presentation.

These spectacular desserts make entertaining easy in a very basic way. Serve them at the end of an otherwise simply prepared menu, and they leave your guests with the lasting impression that the meal has been an extravaganza. That's what a grand finale is all about.

Pavlova with Raspberries, Passion Fruit and Glass Bark (recipe page 78)

6 egg whites

pinch of salt

2$^1/_4$ cups (18 oz/565 g) superfine (castor) sugar

2 teaspoons distilled white vinegar

1 teaspoon vanilla extract (essence), or to taste

1$^1/_4$ cups (10 fl oz/310 ml) heavy (double) cream

4 passion fruits

2 cups (8 oz/250 g) raspberries

PAVLOVA WITH RASPBERRIES, PASSION FRUIT AND GLASS BARK

The meringue shell and glass bark of this stunning creation can be made up to 3 days ahead and stored in airtight containers. Use any fresh, juicy fruit you find in the market. (photograph pages 76–77)

Preheat an oven to 250°F (120°C). To make the meringue, in a large bowl, combine the egg whites and salt and beat until firm, shiny peaks form. Gradually beat in 1$^1/_4$ cups (10 oz/315 g) of the sugar and continue to beat until stiff and glossy. Fold in the vinegar, the vanilla and $^1/_2$ cup (4 oz/125 g) of the remaining sugar.

Cut out a 12-in (30-cm) circle of parchment paper. Wet on one side, shaking off any excess water. Place the paper, damp side up, on a heavy baking sheet. Spoon the egg-white mixture onto the paper, smoothing it out to a 10-in (25-cm) round. Shape the mixture so the sides and top are straight and level. Bake until crisp on the outside and just set in the center, 1$^1/_4$–1$^1/_2$ hours. Carefully remove the paper and let cool on a serving platter.

To make the filling, in a medium bowl, beat the cream until soft peaks form. Spread over the meringue. Scoop out the flesh from the passion fruit and push through a fine-mesh sieve. Stir half of the seeds back into the resulting juice. Drizzle over the Pavlova and then scatter the raspberries over the top.

To make the glass bark, preheat a broiler (griller). Lightly oil the back of a baking sheet and sift the remaining $^1/_2$ cup (4 oz/125 g) sugar over it. Broil until melted and golden. Watch the sugar carefully as it burns quickly. Let cool.

Place a sheet of parchment paper on a work surface. Tap the baking sheet hard over the paper, so that the glass bark falls off in shards. Break into pieces and stick into the top of the Pavlova. Cut into wedges and serve.

SERVES 8

3 egg yolks plus 1 egg white

3 tablespoons superfine
  (castor) sugar

1¹/₃ cups (11 fl oz/330 ml)
  Marsala or brandy

¹/₄ cup (2 fl oz/60 ml)
  very strong espresso

8 oz (250 g) mascarpone,
  at room temperature

¹/₂ cup (4 fl oz/125 ml) heavy
  (double) cream

4 oz (125 g) ladyfingers

TIRAMISÙ

The name of this Tuscan trifle translates as "pick me up"—an apt description for the effect the layered concoction of zabaglione custard, mascarpone cheese and ladyfingers has on guests. It should be made at least several hours ahead of time and can be prepared the night before. Some cooks like to dust the top with cocoa powder or chocolate shavings. (photograph page 19)

In the top of a double boiler, beat the egg yolks and sugar until ivory-colored. Add ¹/₃ cup (3 fl oz/80 ml) of the Marsala or brandy and whisk over gently simmering water until the mixture begins to thicken into a custard. Let cool.

In a small bowl, stir together the espresso and mascarpone. In a medium bowl, whip the cream until soft peaks form. In a small bowl, beat the egg white until stiff. Fold the egg white into the yolk-sugar mixture. Dip the ladyfingers into the remaining 1 cup (8 fl oz/250 ml) Marsala or brandy and arrange in a single layer in the bottom of a 9-in (23-cm) bowl. Cover with half of the mascarpone, then half of the custard and half of the whipped cream. Repeat the layers, finishing with the whipped cream. Refrigerate for several hours before serving on individual plates.

SERVES 6

6 pears, preferably Comice
or Anjou

3 cups (24 fl oz/750 ml)
Pinot Noir wine

1$^1/_3$ cups (11 oz/340 g) sugar

6 egg yolks

$^3/_4$ cup (6 fl oz/180 ml)
crème de cacao

1 tablespoon unsweetened
cocoa powder

$^1/_2$ cup (4 oz/125 g) crème fraîche
or sour cream

POACHED PEARS WITH CHOCOLATE SABAYON

The luxurious, ruby-tinted pears, complemented by a rich and airy chocolate custard, make a spectacular ending to a gala dinner. You can cook the pears up to a day ahead and refrigerate them in their poaching liquid; before serving, reduce the liquid to a syrup and prepare the sabayon. A chilled glass of pear brandy is the perfect companion. If you like, garnish with strips of orange zest.

Peel the pears and core them from the bottom, leaving the stems intact. In a medium nonreactive saucepan over low heat, combine the pears, the Pinot Noir and 1 cup (8 oz/250 g) of the sugar. Add water to cover and simmer until the pears are tender, 30–40 minutes. Transfer the pears to a large bowl. Raise the heat to medium and cook the poaching liquid until it is reduced to a syrup, 30–45 minutes. Ladle the syrup over the pears.

To make the chocolate sabayon, in a double boiler over gently simmering water, combine the egg yolks, liqueur, cocoa and the remaining $^1/_3$ cup (3 oz/ 90 g) sugar. Whisk until the mixture is light and fluffy.

To serve, place the pears in glasses or on plates, pour the Pinot Noir syrup over the top and drizzle with the chocolate sabayon, then the crème fraîche or sour cream.

SERVES 6

$^1/_2$ cup (2$^1/_2$ oz/75 g) flour

pinch of salt

4 eggs

1$^1/_2$ cups (12 fl oz/375 ml) milk

3 tablespoons unsalted butter

2 tablespoons Cognac or brandy

cherry or apricot jam

sugar

PROVENÇAL CRÊPES

A favorite dessert in France, crêpes could not be simpler, making a great dessert for a Sunday brunch. They are made in pans the size of dinner plates and presented at the table with a choice of jams (cherry and apricot are favorites), sugar and, often, a bottle of génépi, a strong herbal liqueur for which Cognac or brandy can be substituted. Each guest flavors the crêpes to taste before rolling them up.

In a large bowl, stir together the flour and salt. Make a well in the center and add the eggs. Whisk, working gradually from the center of the bowl outward, until no lumps remain. If the mixture begins to become pasty, add a little milk. Slowly whisk in the milk and continue to whisk until the batter is the consistency of light cream. If the batter is not completely smooth, pass it through a sieve into another bowl. In a crêpe pan or a 9-in (23-cm) sauté pan over low heat, melt the butter. Pour the butter into the batter along with the Cognac or brandy. Stir to mix.

Wipe the pan, leaving only a film of butter. Heat the pan over medium heat, then reduce the heat to medium-low. Stir the batter with a small ladle, lift the pan and, while rotating it, pour in just enough batter to coat the bottom and edges of the pan. The batter should sizzle on contact. Return the pan to the heat. Cook until the surface of the crêpe is nearly dry and the edges turn golden and curl away from the pan, 1–2 minutes. Slip a round-tipped knife blade beneath the crêpe and flip it over. A few seconds later, transfer it to a heated plate.

Remove the pan from the heat for 2–3 seconds before adding batter for the next crêpe. Briefly stir the batter with the ladle each time before pouring. Do not butter the pan; the butter contained in the batter is sufficient. Stack the crêpes as they come out of the pan and serve while still warm, accompanied by the jam and sugar.

SERVES 4

1 cup (8 oz/250 g) unsalted butter, at room temperature

2 cups (6 oz/185 g) unsweetened cocoa powder

6 oz (185 g) bittersweet (plain) chocolate, broken into $^1/_2$-in (12-mm) pieces

1 cup (8 fl oz/250 ml) heavy (double) cream

8 large egg yolks

$^3/_4$ cup (6 oz/185 g) sugar

$^1/_4$ cup (2 fl oz/60 ml) Scotch whiskey

2 lb (1 kg) frozen sweetened raspberries, thawed, puréed and sieved

1 tablespoon cornstarch (cornflour)

$^1/_4$ cup (2 fl oz/60 ml) raspberry liqueur or brandy

CHOCOLATE PÂTÉ WITH RASPBERRY SAUCE

Serve this at the end of a very elegant dinner or a party honoring a confirmed chocoholic. The exceptionally good dessert, adapted from a recipe by John Bishop, needs to be made the day before serving and can be frozen for up to 1 month. Garnish with fresh raspberries and strips of orange zest, if you like.

Line the long sides and bottom of an 8$^1/_2$-by-4$^1/_2$-in (21.5-by-11.5-cm) loaf pan with a sheet of parchment paper, allowing the paper to extend 3 in (7.5 cm) over each side. Brush the paper and insides of the pan with oil.

To make the pâté, in a medium bowl, combine the butter and cocoa and beat until very smooth. In a double boiler over barely simmering water, melt the chocolate, stirring constantly. Let cool. In a large bowl, whip the cream until stiff peaks form. In a large bowl, combine the egg yolks and sugar. Beat until the mixture is thick and pale yellow, 3–5 minutes. Add the melted chocolate to the egg mixture and beat until well blended. Add the butter-cocoa mixture and beat until smooth. Stir in the Scotch whiskey, then gently fold in the whipped cream. Transfer to the loaf pan and smooth the top with a spatula. Gently tap the pan to eliminate any air bubbles. Cover and freeze overnight.

To make the raspberry sauce, place the raspberry purée in a medium sauce-pan. In a small bowl, dissolve the cornstarch in the liqueur or brandy. Stir into the raspberry purée. Place over medium heat and cook, stirring constantly, until the sauce comes to a boil and thickens. Let cool.

To serve, remove the chocolate pâté from the freezer and let sit at room temperature for 30 minutes. Run a knife along each short side of the pan and lift the pâté out by the paper wings. Invert on a serving platter, carefully peel off the paper and surround with some of the raspberry sauce. Spoon 2 table-spoons of the sauce on each individual plate. With a knife dipped in hot water, cut the pâté into $^1/_2$-in (12-mm) slices and place a slice on each plate.

SERVES 16

CHOCOLATE-RASPBERRY CREAM PUFFS WITH PRALINE POWDER

1 cup (8 fl oz/250 ml) water

$^1/_2$ cup (4 oz/125 g) unsalted butter

1 cup (5 oz/155 g) flour

4 eggs

1 cup (6 oz/185 g) semisweet (plain) chocolate chips

6 oz (185 g) cream cheese, at room temperature

$^1/_2$ cup (2 oz/60 g) confectioners' (icing) sugar

1 tablespoon raspberry-flavored liqueur

$^1/_2$ cup (4 fl oz/125 ml) heavy (double) cream

$^1/_2$ cup (4 oz/125 g) granulated sugar

$^1/_2$ cup ($2^1/_2$ oz/75 g) almonds or macadamia nuts, lightly toasted (see page 14)

$1^1/_2$ cups (6 oz/185 g) raspberries, puréed and sieved

raspberries and blueberries

Cream puffs make such an impressive dessert that few people realize how simple they are to make and how much of the work can be done ahead. The puffs and praline powder may be made up to 3 days in advance and stored at room temperature in airtight containers; the chocolate-raspberry filling may be prepared and refrigerated the day before. Assemble the dessert no more than 2 hours before serving, for the best texture.

Preheat an oven to 400°F (200°C). To make the cream puffs, in a medium saucepan over low heat, combine the water and butter. Bring to a boil and remove from the heat. Add the flour and stir vigorously until the mixture forms a ball and leaves a film on the sides of the pan. Cool slightly, 3–4 minutes. Add the eggs, one at a time, beating well after each addition. Drop 2 rounded tablespoonfuls of dough onto an ungreased baking sheet, forming mounds spaced about 2 in (5 cm) apart. You should have enough dough for 20 cream puffs. Bake until puffed and golden, 35–40 minutes. Let cool on the baking sheet.

To make the chocolate-raspberry cream, in the top pan of a double boiler over gently simmering water, melt the chocolate chips, stirring constantly until smooth. In a medium bowl, combine the cream cheese, confectioners' sugar and liqueur and beat until creamy. Gradually add the melted chocolate, beating well. In a medium bowl, beat the cream until stiff peaks form. Fold the cream into the chocolate mixture until just blended. Cover and refrigerate.

To make the praline powder, in a heavy sauté pan over medium-low heat, melt the granulated sugar, stirring constantly. When the sugar has turned to liquid and is light brown, stir in the almonds or macadamias. Pour the nuts onto a large buttered plate and let cool. When cool, break into pieces and place in a food processor fitted with the metal blade. Process until crumbly.

To assemble the cream puffs, slice the cream puffs in half horizontally. Fill the bottoms with the cream filling. Replace the tops.

To serve, ladle the puréed raspberries onto individual plates and set the puffs on the purée. Drizzle the cream puffs with any remaining cream filling and sprinkle liberally with the praline powder. Garnish each plate with raspberries and blueberries.

SERVES 10

3 egg whites

3 cups (12 oz/375 g) confectioners' (icing) sugar

1 cup (8 fl oz/250 ml) heavy (double) cream

7 oz (220 g) semisweet (plain) chocolate

$^1/_2$ cup (4 fl oz/125 ml) milk

MERINGUES AND CREAM WITH CHOCOLATE SAUCE

Simplicity itself, this favorite dessert from Italy's Piedmont region transforms a casual dinner with friends into a memorable occasion. You can make the meringues up to 2 days ahead and store them in an airtight container at room temperature, to be assembled with freshly whipped cream shortly before serving.

Preheat an oven to 250°F (120°C). In a medium bowl, whip the egg whites, gradually adding the confectioners' sugar, until very stiff and glossy peaks form. Butter and flour a baking sheet. Spoon the meringue into a pastry bag fitted with a large plain tip and squeeze mounds of the mixture about 2 in (5 cm) in diameter, about 3 in (7.5 cm) apart, on the baking sheet. You should have enough whipped eggs for 12 meringues. Bake until hardened but still white, about 30 minutes. Transfer to a rack to cool.

In a medium bowl, whip the cream until soft peaks form. Spread the whipped cream on the bottom of one of the meringues. Place the bottom of another meringue on the cream. Repeat with the remaining meringues until they are all joined in pairs. In the top pan of a double boiler over simmering water, melt the chocolate with the milk, stirring to combine.

To serve, pour the chocolate sauce into a pitcher. Arrange the meringues on a serving plate and accompany with the sauce.

SERVES 6

5 egg yolks

²/₃ cup (5 oz/150 g) sugar

2 cups (16 fl oz/500 ml) heavy
(double) cream

8–14 rose geranium leaves
(see page 13)

³/₄ cup (3 oz/90 g) blueberries

BLUEBERRY CRÈME BRÛLÉE WITH ROSE GERANIUM

San Antonio chef Kim Swendson-Cameron created this elegant-but-easy garden-party recipe. In an unusual touch, she tucks blueberries beneath the caramelized crust and flavors the custard with rose geranium. You could use any of the many other varieties of scented geranium leaves, including lemon, lime, apple, peppermint, apricot, peach or even nutmeg. If you grow your own, be sure to pick the leaves early in the morning for maximum flavor. (photograph page 27)

Preheat an oven to 325°F (165°C). In a large bowl, whisk together the egg yolks and ¹/₃ cup (2¹/₂ oz/75 g) of the sugar until the sugar dissolves and the mixture is a light lemon color. In a medium saucepan over medium heat, combine the cream and 2 of the rose geranium leaves and heat gently to just under a boil. Remove from the heat. Remove and discard the leaves. Whisk 1–2 tablespoons of the cream into the egg mixture, then gradually whisk the egg mixture into the cream.

Place 2 tablespoons of the blueberries in the bottom of each of 6 ramekins with a ¹/₂–²/₃ cup (4–5 fl oz/125–160 ml) capacity. Set them in a baking pan. Divide the custard evenly among the ramekins. Pour boiling water into the baking pan to reach halfway up the sides of the ramekins. Bake until the custard is set and a knife inserted in the center comes out clean, about 25 minutes. Let cool in the water bath, then remove from the water bath, cover and refrigerate until thoroughly chilled, at least 4 hours or as long as 2 days.

To serve, preheat a broiler (griller). Evenly dust the tops of the custards with the remaining ¹/₃ cup (2¹/₂ oz/75 g) sugar. Place under the broiler until the sugar caramelizes, 1–3 minutes. Remove from the broiler, let cool slightly and garnish each serving with 1 or 2 rose geranium leaves.

SERVES 6

1/4 cup (2 oz/60 g) unsalted butter

1 cup (7 oz/220 g) lightly packed
light brown sugar

1/2 teaspoon ground cinnamon

1/4 cup (2 fl oz/60 ml)
banana liqueur

4 bananas, cut in half lengthwise
and then crosswise

1/4 cup (2 fl oz/60 ml) dark rum

1 qt (1 l) vanilla ice cream

BRENNAN'S BANANAS FOSTER

In 1951, New Orleans restaurateur Edward Brennan asked chef Paul Blange to prepare a little something sweet for breakfast, and Blange named his now-legendary creation for a devoted patron, businessman Richard Foster. Bananas Foster is traditionally prepared tableside so guests can admire the final step of flambéing. Served at home, it makes an impressive conclusion to a brunch party.

In a 10-in (25-cm) flambé or sauté pan over low heat either on an alcohol burner or on top of a gas stove, combine the butter, brown sugar and cinnamon. Cook, stirring, until the sugar has dissolved and the butter has melted. Stir in the banana liqueur, then place the bananas in the pan. Cook until the banana sections soften, turning them to brown on both sides, about 6 minutes total. Pour in the rum and cook until the rum is hot, about 1 minute. Carefully tip the pan very slightly to the side to just catch a tiny bit of the burner flame in the pan and ignite the rum. Immediately straighten the pan upright. Do not move the pan; let it stand until the flames cease.

To serve, scoop the vanilla ice cream into 4 individual dishes. Place 4 pieces of banana on the ice cream. Spoon the warm sauce over the top.

SERVES 4

2 cups (10 oz/310 g) flour

1 tablespoon baking powder

¹/₄ teaspoon salt

2 tablespoons sugar

1 tablespoon ground cinnamon

1¹/₃ cups (11 fl oz/330 ml) milk

4 eggs, separated

1 tablespoon vegetable oil

1 tablespoon lemon juice

2 cups (12 oz/375 g) Bing cherries, pitted

oil, for frying

sifted confectioners' (icing) sugar

18–24 Bing cherries, unpitted

BING CHERRY FRITTERS

You can use almost any of your favorite fruits in place of the cherries, making this a year-round spectacular ending for a party at any time of day, from breakfast to after a show. The batter mixes in minutes, ready to fry the fruit, which is dusted with confectioners' sugar and served hot, crisp and golden.

Into a large bowl, sift together the flour, baking powder, salt, sugar and cinnamon. Add the milk, egg yolks, 1 tablespoon oil and lemon juice and beat until smooth. In a large bowl, whip the egg whites until soft peaks form, then gently fold them into the batter. Fold in the pitted cherries.

In a deep, heavy saucepan over high heat, pour oil to a depth of 3 in (7.5 cm) and heat to 375° (190°C) on a deep-fat thermometer. Drop the batter by tablespoonfuls into the hot oil and fry until golden brown, 3–5 minutes. Drain on paper towels and keep warm in a very low oven. Repeat until all the batter is cooked. Serve at once, topped with confectioners' sugar and garnished with cherries.

SERVES 6

1 cup (8 oz/250 g) unsalted butter

2 cups (8 oz/250 g) coarsely
  chopped, peeled apples

2 cups (8 oz/250 g) pecans or
  walnuts, toasted (see page 14)

1¾ cups (14 oz/440 g) sugar

¼ cup (1½ oz/45 g) golden
  raisins (sultanas)

1 teaspoon finely grated
  lemon zest

4 tablespoons lemon juice

2 teaspoons ground cinnamon

½ lb (250 g) filo sheets,
  each about 14 by 18 in
  (35.5 by 45.5 cm)

1¼ cups (10 fl oz/310 ml) water

½ cup (6 oz/185 g) honey

½ teaspoon ground cinnamon

2 or 3 whole cloves

APPLE STRUDEL BAKLAVA

This luscious dessert, created by Cynthia Pedregon for the Peach Tree Tea Room in Fredericksburg, Texas, is an imaginative marriage of Viennese and Middle Eastern favorites. It will take you a couple of hours to assemble and bake the layered pastry, but it keeps well in the refrigerator for several days or in the freezer for up to 1 month. Serve it for a special morning coffee or afternoon tea, garnished with pomegranate seeds and strips of lemon zest.

In a small saucepan over low heat, melt the butter. Remove from the heat and let stand for a few minutes, then skim off and discard the white foam that rises to the top. Pour off the clear yellow liquid (the clarified butter) into a small bowl, leaving the milky residue in the bottom of the pan. Set aside.

Preheat an oven to 350°F (180°C). In a large bowl, combine the apples, the pecans or walnuts, ½ cup (4 oz/125 g) of the sugar, the raisins, the lemon zest and juice and the 2 teaspoons cinnamon. Toss to mix thoroughly.

Carefully unroll the filo sheets onto a clean work surface. Cut the stack in half lengthwise to form 2 stacks each about 9 by 14 in (23 by 35.5 cm). Cover with plastic wrap and a damp towel to prevent drying.

Brush the bottom and sides of a 9-by-13-in (23-by-33-cm) baking dish with the melted butter. Lay 1 filo sheet in the dish and brush with butter. Repeat with 5 more sheets, brushing each with butter. Spread half of the apple filling over the pastry. Top with 4 more filo sheets, buttering each sheet well. Spread with the remaining apple mixture. Top with the remaining filo sheets, again buttering each sheet. When all of the sheets are in the dish, brush the top with butter. Using a very sharp knife, cut into diamonds about 1½ by 2 in (4 by 5 cm). Bake until golden, about 45 minutes. Let cool in the pan.

To make the syrup, in a small saucepan over medium-high heat, combine the water, honey, $1/2$ teaspoon cinnamon, cloves and remaining $1^{1}/_{4}$ cups (10 oz/ 315 g) sugar. Bring to a boil, stirring to dissolve the sugar. Reduce the heat to low and simmer until thickened, about 10 minutes. Remove from the heat and remove and discard the cloves. Let cool, then pour evenly over the top of the baklava.

To serve, run a sharp knife along the previously made cuts, lift out the baklava pieces and arrange on a large serving platter or or individual plates.

SERVES 20

ACKNOWLEDGMENTS

Recipes and photographs in *Festive Desserts* first appeared in the following *Beautiful Cookbooks.*

RECIPES

Australia the Beautiful Cookbook, copyright © 1995, pages 47, 78. *California the Beautiful Cookbook,* copyright © 1991, pages 25, 33, 39, 52. *France the Beautiful Cookbook,* copyright © 1989, pages 61, 73, 74. *Italy the Beautiful Cookbook,* copyright © 1988, pages 79, 88. *Mediterranean the Beautiful Cookbook,* copyright © 1994, pages 65, 68. *Pacific Northwest the Beautiful Cookbook,* copyright © 1993, pages 22, 23, 29, 42, 43, 44, 50, 67, 80, 85, 91. *Provence the Beautiful Cookbook,* copyright © 1993, pages 40, 49, 82. *The South the Beautiful Cookbook,* copyright © 1996, pages 30, 34, 53, 55, 57, 69, 70, 75, 90. *Texas the Beautiful Cookbook,* copyright © 1995, pages 26, 62, 64, 66, 86, 89, 92.

PHOTOGRAPHY

E. Jane Armstrong, copyright © 1993, pages 1, 2, 28, 45, 51, 67, 82, 84, 91; copyright © 1995, pages 27, 63, 66, 87, 93. **Peter Johnson**, copyright © 1989, pages 60, 72; copyright © 1993, pages 41, 48, 83; copyright © 1994, pages 58–59; copyright © 1995, pages 46, 76–77. **Allan Rosenberg,** copyright © 1991, pages 8, 24, 32, 38; copyright © 1996, pages 6–7, 15, 16, 19, 20–21, 94. **Philip Salaverry,** copyright © 1996, pages 31, 35, 36–37, 54, 56, 71, 90.

INDEX